# THE SE( COTSW(

C000319668

*Exploring the Cotswolds with*
*10 original tours and unusual places to visit*

# Julia Owen

S.B. Publications

First published in 1995 by S.B. Publications
c/o 19 Grove Road, Seaford, East Sussex BN25 1TP

ISBN 1 85770 080 5

Typeset and printed by Island Press Ltd.
3 Cradle Hill Industrial Estate, Seaford, East Sussex BN25 3JE
Telephone: 01323 490222 UK

# CONTENTS

*Front cover:* Keble's Bridge at Eastleach
*Back cover:* Late 12th century carved porch, St. Swithin's Church, Quenington

# INTRODUCTION

On the face of it nowhere could seem less secret than the Cotswolds. Picturesque images of golden stone villages nestling among gentle sheep-covered hills grace the covers of countless calendars or chocolate boxes: here is the advertiser's dream of a perfect England, unmodernised, uncommercialised and untainted by modern life.

In the summer months coachloads of tourists arrive at the better known Cotswold beauty spots, cameras clicking, video recorders whirring. There is all the business of souvenirs and tearooms, busy car parks and traffic jams. the locals breathe a sigh of relief when the last of the tourist buses depart; you won't find them among the crowds at Bourton-on-the-Water on a Bank Holiday Monday, or in Broadway on a busy August weekend. They know dozens of equally enchanting villages which lie just off the beaten track, perfect picnic spots beside slow moving trout-filled streams, and wonderful pubs with log fires and real ale. This book aims to share the secrets of this beautiful part of Britain.

Many people have differing ideas as to the exact size of the Cotswolds, some include great chunks of Oxfordshire and Wiltshire, others think of Cheltenham and Gloucester and the area right up to the River Severn as Cotswold country. Officially speaking, the Cotswolds covers an area of 790 square miles and is designated as an Area of Outstanding Natural Beauty. It stretches from Chipping Campden in the north to the outskirts of Bath in the south.

It is safe to say that you will know when you are in the Cotswolds; there is something about the landscape that is unique. Witney likes to think of itself as a Cotswold town, but it is only when you cross the invisible boundary a few miles east of Burford that you realise that it is not. The geography of the area with its massive limestone escarpment running down the western side of the region and the gentle slope eastwards, gives the area its unmistakable characteristics: the colour of the stone, the contours of its low hills and narrow streams.

Coming back to the Cotswolds after an absence of ten years offered the chance to see the area with a fresh perspective. After living in Moscow and Brussels and the Middle East, the Cotswolds seemed unbelievably beautiful. I wanted to find out everything about the area where I had grown up and was now returning to with my family: these explorations led to the writing of this book. We drove hundreds of miles over twisting country roads, spending memorable days seeking out Norman fonts, real Cotswold sheep or

Roman remains. Our days out often had themes and it is these excursions which form the basis of this book.

Each of the ten tours in this book will take you through a different part of the secret Cotswolds. You could easily cover the ground of each tour in a morning since the average distance is between 20 and 40 miles, but the excursions are designed to fill a full day out. I have included recommendations for places to stop for lunch or refreshment as well as practical information on nearby attractions. One of the main aims is to keep off busy main roads as far as is realistically possible. This does mean that some of the suggested routes are on very minor roads and particular care should be taken. Do check opening hours of attractions you particularly want to see: some open for only a few hours each week, some close all winter. The sketch maps included in the book are not drawn to scale and are only to give you a rough idea of the route; a good map will add immeasurably to the pleasure of your excursion.

# THE AUTHOR

Julia Owen grew up in the Cotswolds and was educated in Cheltenham and at University College, London. After spending ten years abroad with her journalist husband in Moscow, Brussels and the Middle East, she has returned to live in the Cotswolds with her three children. As a freelance travel writer she has contributed articles to numerous newspapers and magazines.

# KEY TO TOURS

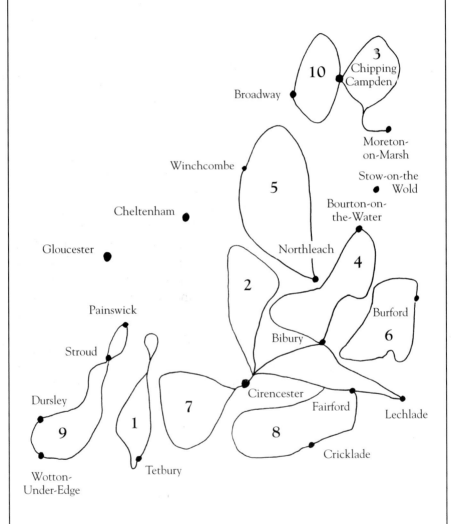

# 1. ROYAL CONNECTIONS

The Cotswolds are resonant with royal connections both ancient and modern. There was King Caractacus, the ancient Briton, who is said to have gone to ground near Minchinhampton after his defeat by the Romans, and William the Conqueror who spent Christmas with his court at Gloucester and ordered the Domesday Book while his Queen Matilda sorrowfully built the church at Avening. Edward II was buried at Gloucester, Henry VIII and most of his wives stayed at Sudeley Castle at one time or another. The forces of King Charles battled it out with Oliver Cromwell through some of the bloodiest battles of the Civil War. The Prince Regent started a craze for Cotswold spa water at Cheltenham, and no less than three of the present day young royals have chosen the area for their country retreats. There is quite a case for renaming the area the Royal County of Gloucestershire.

We begin our tour in Tetbury, a perfect example of a Cotswold market town. It became rich with the wool trade, and despite its subsequent decline it has preserved its picturesque charm.

# TOUR 1 – ROYAL CONNECTIONS

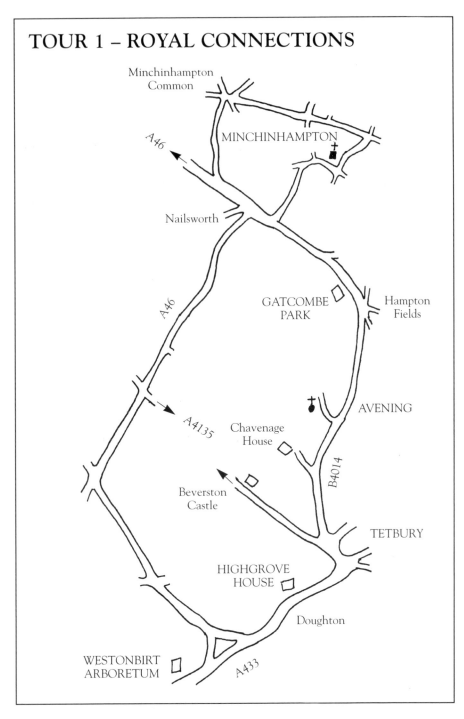

# DIRECTIONS:

*After visiting Tetbury take the B4014 north to Avening. Turn left at the Cross Inn to visit the Avening church, but return to this junction and take the other turning (to your left now) at the pub. Take the left fork at Hampton Fields to Minchinhampton. At the crossroads in Minchinhampton village turn right into the Market Square, and bear right again at the war memorial down Butts Lane. At the end of this lane there is a cross roads – turn left towards Minchinhampton Common. Drive into the centre of the common and pick up the sign post to Nailsworth. At Nailsworth turn left onto the A46. After crossing the A4135 take the first left – this will bring you across to the A433 at the Hare & Hounds pub at Westonbirt. Turn right to visit the Arboretum, or left to return through the hamlet of Doughton to Tetbury.*

# APPROX. DISTANCE: *22 miles*

# RECOMMENDED:

*The Snooty Fox Hotel, The Close Hotel, The Crown Inn, Tetbury Gallery Tea Room, Tetbury; The Bell Inn, Avening; The Crown Inn, Minchinhampton; Calcot Manor, Beverston; The Hare & Hounds, Westonbirt.*

TETBURY is a delightful small market town with typical high-gabled Cotswold houses clustered around the picturesque market place. Never really busy except on Wednesdays when the antiques market is held upstairs in the 17th century beamed market hall and the stall holders are in full swing below selling local produce and plants, Tetbury is the ideal royal bolthole. The speciality shops are particularly delectable and you will need a whole day just to browse in the antique shops all the way up Long Street. Several of the shops boast the coveted silver feathers of Prince Charles's warrant which are proudly displayed above the shopfronts.

The origins of the town go back to around 1200 and are apparent in the medieval layout of the streets and the quaint names like Gumstool Hill where the riotous Woolsack races are held on Spring Bank Holiday Mondays, the object being to manhandle a 65lb wool sack between two pubs, the Royal Oak and the Crown, down the steep hill and back again. Gumstool Hill once had a pond at the bottom of it where scolding wives and minor offenders were punished with a ducking in the water on a 'gumstool'.

Tetbury's wealth came with the wool trade. It was already a thriving market town when the Market Hall with its unusual dolphin weathervane

*17th century Market Hall and The Snooty Fox Hotel, Tetbury.*

4

was built in 1655. The wool was weighed and sold here. Chipping Steps was the site of the old Mop Fair where labourers and farmhands, domestic servants and craftsmen assembled, clutching emblems of their trade, each with the aim of attracting a new employer. 'Chipping' was the old word for a market, as in Chipping Campden or Chipping Norton.

The parish church of St. Mary was one of the first Gothic Revival churches, designed and built by Francis Hiorn in 1781. Recent restoration work at a cost of £500,000 has stripped the church of its Victorian additions and revealed the cool elegance of the Georgian building.

Just north of Tetbury we have a royal connection at the village of Avening and we make a short detour to visit the historic Norman church. Queen Matilda (who is remembered in the town arms 'MAT(ILDA) 1080 REG(INA)', wife of William the Conqueror, built the beautiful and atmospheric church dedicated to the Holy Rood or Cross in 1080. it is a tale of unrequited love, and royal remorse.

Before the Conquest Avening belonged to Brittric, Lord of Gloucester, who met Matilda while on an important embassy to Baldwin, Duke of Flanders. Matilda was smitten with great love for the handsome Brittric, but he refused to marry her, and in pique she married William, Duke of Normandy. As soon as

*Royal Warrant, Tetbury*

5

*Avening Church.*

Britain had fallen to the Norman conquerors, Matilda arrived in Avening on the arm of the new King of England. Brittric was thrown into prison and died soon afterwards. Matilda had married in haste, now she repented at leisure and built the fine church at Avening in penance. Meanwhile, her husband was busy with the Domesday Book, ordered while the court spent Christmas at Gloucester in 1085.

It is just possible to glimpse GATCOMBE PARK, the country home of the Princess Royal, from the top of Avening Hill but there are several opportunities each year to take a closer look at the grounds. The house is not open to the public. In late August for example the grounds are opened for the famous British Open Horse Trials Championship for a 3 day event in which the country's top eventers compete over a course designed by Mark Phillips. There are stands, bands, gun dog trials, parachute spectaculars and fly fishing competitions to keep everyone entertained. (Details from The Horse Trials Office, Badminton. Tel: 01454-218272). There are also twice yearly rounds of Novice Horse Trials at Gatcombe in the autumn and spring and regular Craft Fairs in the grounds.

The Queen gave Gatcombe Park to Princess Anne and Mark Phillips as a wedding present in 1976. It is a fairly small house of 32 rooms, but beautifully and discreetly set into the side of the wooded valley. Built in 1771-4 for Samuel

Sheppard who was High Sheriff of the county, it was added to in the 1820s by George Basevi, architect of Cambridge's Fitzwilliam Museum.

We continue north through MINCHINHAMPTON, which has an interesting church and a delightful market place. It also has an extensive common with magnificent views where you can explore the BULWARKS, a series of Iron Age earthworks. From the car it is hard to sort out the golf greens and bunkers from the mounds and ditches, but they are extraordinarily impressive. It is thought that these fortifications were the work of a local Belgic tribe who took a desperate stand against the Romans in the first century. King Cunobelinus, the subject of Shakespeare's play *Cymbeline*, left his territory to his two sons, one of whom made a treaty with the invaders. The other, our royal connection here, was King Caractacus, who suffered a terrible defeat in AD43 but withdrew to Minchinhampton to regroup with the warlike Welsh tribes who came to his aid.

We come back through NAILSWORTH, a small town on a steep hill. Its steepest hill is the picturesque Nailsworth Ladder.

Cutting across from the A46 we come out onto the A433 Tetbury to Bath road at the Hare & Hounds pub by WESTONBIRT ARBORETUM (Open daily 10.00-8.00 or sunset if earlier. Admission Charge. Tel: 01666-880220). Now owned by the Forestry Commission it lies directly opposite Westonbirt

*Entrance gates, Highgrove House.*

7

School, a girls public school housed in the magnificent Elizabethan-style house built for Robert Holford by Lewis Vulliamy in 1863-70. Vulliamy had previously built Dorchester House in Park Lane as Holford's London residence. The 600 acre Arboretum with its 17 miles of forest trails was part of the original garden. Visitors come from all over the world to see the incredible autumn colours, but Westonbirt is beautiful at all times of the year.

The hamlet of DOUGHTON straddles a double bend on the main road back to Tetbury. HIGHGROVE HOUSE  is hidden from view behind high stone walls and a pair of wrought iron gates, which were presented to Prince Charles as a wedding present by the people of Tetbury. Prince Charles bought Highgrove in 1980, the year before his marriage, from Maurice Macmillan, son of Prime Minister Harold Macmillan. It had been built in 1798 for John Paul Paul, descendent of a Huguenot family who had made a fortune in the woollen industry. Highgrove House and its grounds are not open to the public.

Within easy reach of Tetbury you could visit CHAVENAGE HOUSE (Open May-Sept, Thurs, Sun + Bank Hol Mons only, 2.00-5.00. Admission Charge. Tel: 01666-502329) with its fine collection of 17th century tapestries and furniture. During the Civil War siege of nearby Beaverston Castle in 1644, Cromwell stayed at the Elizabethan manor house which has a room named after him and another after Ireton. The impressive ruins of 13th century BEVERSTON CASTLE are clearly visible from the lane leading up to the charming Norman church at Beverston but they are not open to the public.

## FURTHER EXPLORATION:

Beautiful SUDELEY CASTLE near Winchcombe is the principal Cotswold attraction with royal connections (SEE TOUR 5).

Edward II, who was murdered in Berkeley Castle, was buried in GLOUCESTER CATHEDRAL in 1337. The magnificent tomb erected by his son Edward III became an important place of pilgrimage throughout the Middle Ages.

# 2. FRIENDS, ROMANS, COUNTRYMEN!

There is much truth in the old saying 'Scratch Gloucestershire and find Rome': you don't even have to scratch very deeply, since you are probably on a Roman road already. Cirencester or *Corinium*, stands at the major Roman road junctions of Akeman Street, Ermin Street and the Fosse Way.

Nearly a hundred years after Julius Caesar's army first landed on the Kent coast in 54BC, Aulus Plautius set off with a serious expeditionary force of some 50,000 men and a number of elephants to conquer Britain. Within three or four years the Roman forces commanded half of the country, the half to the east of the Fosse Way.

This great road which runs right through the Cotswolds serviced the military frontline of the Roman advance. Protected by a series of forts positioned at strategic intervals, the Fosse Way followed a roughly drawn line from the River Severn to the Humber estuary and linked the towns of Exeter and Lincoln. Cirencester, from its beginnings as a garrison town, grew to be the second largest Roman city in Britain.

Today Cirencester is a delightful bustling market town – medieval in its plan rather than Roman – with a glorious 15th century wool church and a wealth of coaching inns and speciality shops. Possessing one of the finest collections of Roman antiquities in Britain, Cirencester is the natural starting point of our Roman tour.

# TOUR 2 – FRIENDS, ROMANS, COUNTRYMEN!

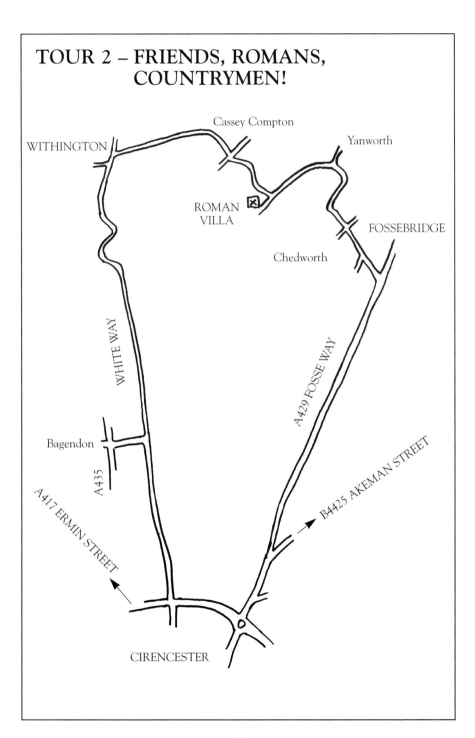

Cassey Compton

Yanworth

WITHINGTON

ROMAN
VILLA

FOSSEBRIDGE

Chedworth

WHITE WAY

A429 FOSSE WAY

Bagendon

A435

B4425 AKEMAN STREET

A417 ERMIN STREET

CIRENCESTER

# DIRECTIONS:

Take the A429 northwards from Cirencester following signs for Stow-on-the-Wold. Go straight across at the large 'Beeches' roundabout and follow the Fosse Way to the left when it joins Akeman Street (B4425 to Burford) after about $1/2$ml. Stay on the A429 for about 6 mls until the hamlet of Fossebridge. Turn left at the bottom of the steep hill just before Fossebridge Inn – there are National Trust signs to the Roman Villa ($3^1/2$mls) from here along the river Coln.

Turn left as you leave the villa and follow the winding valley road through Cassey Compton to Withington. Come into Withington past the small Kings Head pub and turn left (signpost to Cheltenham) into the main village. The Mill Inn is on the right hand side. Just before the church turn left following the signpost to Cirencester – this will bring you up through Withington Woods onto the old White Way and straight back to Cirencester.


# APPROX. DISTANCE: 20 miles


# RECOMMENDED:

The Fleece Inn, The Kings Head Inn, Harry Hare's, Brewery Arts coffee shop, Keith's coffee shop, Cirencester; Fossebridge Inn, Fossebridge; The Mill Inn, Withington.

The TOURIST INFORMATION CENTRE is situated in the Corn Hall on the Market Place at Cirencester. Tel: 01285-654180.

Justly proud of its Roman heritage, CIRENCESTER boasts one of the best collections of Roman art and artifacts in Britain. The award-winning CORINIUM MUSEUM on Park Street (Open daily throughout the year except winter Mondays, Mon-Sat 10.00-5.30, Sun 2.00-5.30pm. Admission Charge. Tel: 01285-655611) offers a fascinating glimpse into everyday Roman life. There is a full-scale reconstruction of a Roman triclinium or dining room complete with mosaic floor, seats to recline on and even menu suggestions for the kitchen. We know the Romans were responsible for bringing pheasants, rabbits, pears, cherries, sweet chestnuts, laurels and apples to Britain. They also brought the enormous edible snail or Helix Pomatia, examples of which can still be spotted ambling around Chedworth woods on wet days.

As well as relics of the two cavalry regiments based in Corinium, including fine tombstones with inscriptions reminding us of the astonishing size and variety of the Roman empire – one soldier, Dannicus came from near Basel in Switzerland – there are the complete contents of an oculists shop found in Cirencester, the famous Christian 'Paternoster' cryptogram and a reconstruction of a mosaic workshop. Over 80 mosaic floors have been excavated locally and the Corinian school of mosaics is known for its pavements depicting the legend of Orpheus, who is generally shown playing his lyre and surrounded by circles of animals and birds carefully drawn from nature. The most famous of these, the 200 square meter Great Orpheus Pavement, lies buried under the churchyard at Woodchester and is uncovered only every ten years or so for public display. But the floors preserved in the Corinium Museum, are no less dazzling and whet one's appetite to see mosaics in a real Roman setting at Chedworth later in our tour.

Before we leave Cirencester we should first inspect some ruins. One of the best kept secrets in Cirencester is the 6,000-seat Roman AMPHITHEATRE. You can make out the bulky outlines of grassed-over tiered seating above the town bypass opposite the new Waitrose supermarket, but it requires perseverance to actually find it. Follow signs for Tetbury and Stroud along Querns Lane, turn left at the T-junction and follow the road past some industrial units and over a bridge above the bypass. Just across this bridge turn immediately right into Cotswold Avenue. The modern housing estate looks unpromising but you will see an English Heritage sign pointing to the amphitheatre or 'bull ring' as it is known locally. (Open all daylight hours. No Admission Charge.).

*Section of the Hunting Dogs Mosaic depicting Neptune, Corinium Museum, Cirencester.*

*Roman Amphitheatre at Cirencester.*

A short section of ROMAN WALL, part of the town's defences, is visible in the Abbey Grounds behind the medieval wool church in the market place. The enormous parish church of St. John the Baptist is one of the glories of the Cotswolds. As you look up at the graceful 162 ft tower you will see the massive buttresses erected when its foundations proved unstable having been dug in an in-filled Roman ditch. It is hard to imagine Roman Cirencester now with its 325 ft basilica, the adjoining market place or forum, and an amphitheatre full of gladiators, and it is tempting to wonder what still lies buried under the town.

As you leave Cirencester pull in for a moment before the big 'Beeches' roundabout and find the plaque on the wall marking the spot of the great Verulamium Gate which stood here at the beginning of the Roman road to St. Alban's. The town had four gates piercing its 2¹/₂ mile defensive walls. According to archaeological speculation the Verulamium gate was extremely grand, with turrets, crenelations and giant ballistas or catapults mounted over the four lane road.

Once on the great Fossse Way you can imagine cohorts of weary Roman soldiers tramping along the straight, straight road. They had probably stopped for rest and recreation in the steam baths and warm mineral springs at Bath before heading off north to conquer the rest of Britain.

*Entrance to Cirencester Parish Church (formerly the Town Hall).*

Fossebridge was one of few places on the Fosse Way where the Romans could water their horses at the road side. The road plunges down the steep hillside to river Coln at the bottom. We leave the Fosse Way turning off left just before the Fossebridge Inn, and follow the picturesque, meandering Coln valley for a couple of miles before crossing the river and gaining higher ground near the Roman villa. This is one of the most beautiful parts of the north Cotswolds and lovely walking country. The Roman villa is well sign posted and before long you will see in the distance the half-timbered guardians cottage and museum with its plume of smoke rising above the pheasant-filled woods. The Romans picked delectable sites for their country houses and nowhere is this more evident than at Chedworth.

CHEDWORTH ROMAN VILLA (Open Mar-Oct, Tues-Sun & Bank Hol Mons 10.00-5.30, Nov-early Dec, Wed-Sun 11.00-4.00. Admission charge. Tel: 01242-890256) is owned by the National Trust, and is undoubtedly the best example of an excavated Roman-British villa in Britain.

It was discovered by accident in 1864 during a house party at nearby Stowell Park when men digging a ferret out of a rabbit hole found pieces of mosaic. The land was owned by the Earl of Eldon who financed the excavation of the villa and built the museum.

Start at the new Visitors Centre and find out exactly what you are looking at. There is an excellent audio-visual presentation and a selection of guide books and souvenirs.

Comfort seems to have been the keyword at Chedworth: efficient

*Chedworth Woods and the Roman Villa.*

underfloor central heating, hot baths, steam rooms, imported marble and of course impressive reception rooms with mosaic floors. Especially interesting is the Four Seasons mosaic, with the figure of Winter in his heavy cloak and thick socks clutching leafless branches in a cold hand, while the enchanting girl representing Spring in the opposite corner, holds a basket of flowers in one hand and has a tiny bird perched on the other. This was very much a luxury villa with all 2nd century AD mod. cons., but its purpose remains something of a mystery. It was obviously the centre of an extensive agricultural estate, but was it also a shrine? The octagonal basin holding 4,700 litres of spring water might have been a shrine to a water goddess, and Christian symbols have been found here: the sheer size and sophistication of the site suggests a deeper purpose.

A narrow road takes us on from the Roman villa through the hamlet of Cassey Compton to the delightful Cotswold village of WITHINGTON. Withington is renowned locally for its welcoming ancient hostelry, The Mill Inn, set on the banks of the Coln river, with blazing fires and restorative food and drink.

Heading back towards Cirencester we turn left just before the church and drive up through Withington Woods, looking out for fallow deer which often leap out onto the road in the most alarming way. We are now on the old White Way, or salt road where pack horses brought the essential mineral down into the Cotswolds. Salt was the only preservative for meat which had to be slaughtered in the Autumn when fodder for the herds became harder to find. The Romans were known to have worked deposits of salt around Droitwich and parts of this road have that Roman straightness that makes one suspect that they had a hand in its construction.

BAGENDON, which was the capital of the local Dobunni tribe in Roman times, list just off to the west of the White Way before you come back down again into Cirencester. The outlines of ancient earthworks are still visible under the fields on the other side of the River Churn above the main A435 road from Cheltenham to Cirencester.

## FURTHER EXPLORATION:

Many of the finds from Bagendon, including early British coins minted on the site, are on display at GLOUCESTER CITY MUSEUM AND ART GALLERY (Brunswick Road, Gloucester. Tel: (01452-524131. Open Mon-Sat 10.00-5.00. Admission Free), as is a fine collection of Roman items from other sites in the area.

Most of the Roman villas in the Cotswold area lie on private land, are unexcavated, and are not open to the public. However the well-preserved GREAT WITCOMBE ROMAN VILLA is open to the public occasionally under the auspices of English Heritage. Details of opening days are available from local Tourist Information Centres.

*North Cerney, north of Bagendon.*

# 3. IN AN ENGLISH COUNTRY GARDEN

The Cotswolds provide an idyllic sheltered setting for some of the most famous and enchanting gardens in the world. You would be entirely justified in spending a whole summer weaving a criss crossed web over the high wolds and deep valleys where some of the greatest gardeners have created their own private paradise.

The grand classic gardens tend to be well organized and welcome the public throughout the year but some shut their gates during the darkest winter months. Most have well stocked specialist nurseries where you can buy your Hidcote lavender or your Kiftsgate rose, they often provide homemade cakes and tea, and all offer a glimpse into another almost lost world of under gardeners, gazebos, hahas and perfect herbaceous borders.

Moreton-in-Marsh would be an excellent starting place for a garden tour. You might need more than one day to see everything you want to as opening hours tend to be idiosyncratic, so do check carefully to see if your itinerary will fit in with the opening times of the gardens you wish to see. Allow plenty of time to savour each garden experience and try to avoid busy Bank Holidays.

# TOUR 3 – ENGLISH COUNTRY GARDEN

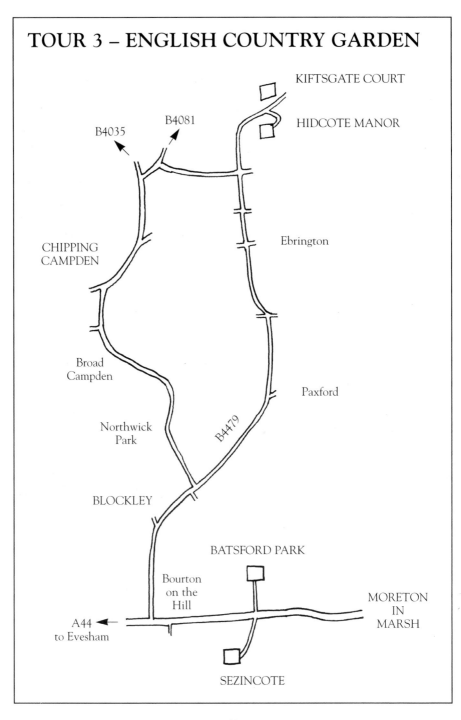

KIFTSGATE COURT

HIDCOTE MANOR

B4081

B4035

CHIPPING
CAMPDEN

Ebrington

Broad
Campden

Paxford

Northwick
Park

B4479

BLOCKLEY

BATSFORD PARK

Bourton
on the
Hill

MORETON
IN
MARSH

A44
to Evesham

SEZINCOTE

# DIRECTIONS:

Leave Moreton-in-Marsh on the A44 road (direction Evesham). After 1ml you will see the entrances to Batsford Park (on right) and Sezincote (on left) opposite each other. Drive on through Bourton-on-the-Hill and at the top of the Hill turn right onto the B4479 to Blockley. Less than 1ml the other side of Blockley turn left following signs for Northwick Business Centre in Northwick Park. Continue through Broad Campden into Chipping Campden where you will see National Trust signs to Hidcote in the town centre. After visiting Chipping Campden follow these signs northwards out of the town, turning right onto B4081 on a sharp bend outside town and almost immediately right again following signs for Hidcote and Kiftsgate (2½mls). Loop back through Ebrington and Paxford where you rejoin the B4479 to Blockley. Turn left at T-junction into Bourton-on-the-Hill and back into Moreton-in-Marsh.

# APPROX. DISTANCE: 25 miles

# RECOMMENDED:

The Redesdale Arms, The Marsh Goose, The Manor House Hotel and The White Hart Royal Hotel at Moreton-in-Marsh; The Crown Inn, Blockley; The Noel Arms Hotel, The Kings Arms Hotel, Chipping Campden; The Ebrington Arms, Ebrington.

MORETON-IN-MARSH is a Fosse Way town at the fording place of the Evenlode river. Its wide market place straddles the main street and is lined with an excellent selection of coaching inns, hotels and eating places, from the luxurious and well-starred to the more basic. People come to the 300 stall Tuesday market from far and wide and almost the entire population turns out for the famous Moreton-in-Marsh agricultural show on the first Saturday each September. It is a real, bustling Cotswold town.

Moreton was known as the Henmarsh in medieval times, a boggy marshland where the wild birds lived. The Curfew Bell on the tower at the corner of Oxford Street was rung daily until as late as 1860, at 5.00am and 8.00pm in the summer and 6.00am and 8.00pm in the winter, to guide travellers through the treacherous marsh. But Moreton was also a railway town. Amazingly the Moreton and Stockton Railway Company was founded in 1821 and the first train, or more precisely horsedrawn wagons on rails, ran five years later. The journey to Paddington now takes a mere 1hr 20mins.

The great champion of the railway at Moreton was Lord Redesdale, grandfather of the famous Mitford sisters, who created the garden at Batsford. As we leave Moreton on the Evesham road, we will see the entrance to Batsford Arboretum directly opposite the driveway to Sezincote, but we will visit Sezincote first, and see Batsford on our way back to Moreton.

SEZINCOTE (Open Thurs, Fri & Bank Hol Mons, 2.00-6.00. Closed December. Admission Charge. Tel: 01386-700444) which John Betjeman dubbed 'the Nabob's house', became the model for Brighton Pavilion following the visit of the Prince Regent in 1807. Sir Charles Cockerell who made his fortune in the East India Company commissioned his brother Samuel Pepys Cockerell to build him an extraordinary house in the Moghul style of architecture. The striking domed house, with its classical 18th century *trompe l'oeil* and muralled interior, is open to the public during summer months (May, June, July & Sept) and is well worth a visit. The exquisite park and oriental water gardens were laid out by landscape architect Humphry Repton and William Daniell, the Indian topographical painter, and include a variety of exotic Eastern trees and plants.

We drive on through the steep and charming village of Bourton-on-the-Hill to Blockley. The road keeps to the edge of the village which is well worth a short detour. BLOCKLEY was the first village in Britain to have electricity; it was also the home of Joanna Southcott (1750-1814), see the plaque outside Rock Cottage, a religious fanatic with a huge following who claimed to receive divinely inspired messages about the Second Coming. Blockley survived the decline of the woollen industry by diversifying into silk; its town mills on the fast flowing streams processed raw silk for the Coventry ribbon trade.

*Thatched cottages and yew hedges, Broad Campden.*

*Entrance to the Ernest Wilson Memorial Garden, Chipping Campden.*

Northwick Park, remodelled by Lord Burlington for the Rushout family in 1730 (now Northwick Business Centre), and its 300 acre grounds are clearly visible from the road as we drive from Blockley towards picture-book BROAD CAMPDEN with its thatched cottages. Broad Campden leads into even more beautiful Chipping Campden.

You must leave the car here and explore this enchanting Cotswold town on foot. CHIPPING CAMPDEN is the most important of the 'Wool Towns' with a massive 15th century cathedral-like 'wool church' and a superb set of alms houses. The fabulously wealthy Sir Baptist Hicks, whose marble effigy you will see in the church, was Lord of the Manor at the time of Charles I and built the great house by the church. Only the gate houses and lodges remain of the mansion which was burnt to the ground during the Civil War.

In the High Street there is the house of an earlier wealthy wool merchant William Grevel (d.1401) with its unique two storey bay window (not open to the public), as well as the house built for another wool merchant, the WOOLSTAPLERS HALL (Open Apr-Oct daily 11.00-6.00. Admission Charge. Tel: 01386-840289) which houses a quaint exhibition of local memorabilia and bric-a-brac. Chipping Campden has a wealth of hotels, quaint pubs, and antique shops. SEE ALSO TOUR 10.

Before leaving you might spare half an hour to pay homage to the ERNEST WILSON MEMORIAL GARDEN (Open daily. No admission charge) at the far end of the town behind the Vicarage. Born in Chipping Campden, the great botanist visited China in 1899 on the first of a series of plant hunting expeditions. He brought back hundreds of previously unknown specimens, some of which can be seen in this delightful garden.

The views over the high Cotswold escarpment are breathtaking as you climb up towards KIFTSGATE COURT (Open April-Sept, Wed, Thurs, Sun & Bank Hol Mons, 2.00-6.00, and June-July, Sats also 2.00-6.00. Admission Charge. Tel: 01386-438777). Kiftsgate, with its dramatic panorama over the Vale of Evesham yet sheltered setting, is the home of the famous Rosa filipes 'Kiftsgate', at 60ft the largest rose in England. In mid-July this luxuriant white rose is a wonder, spralling over a massive copper beech tree. The garden is the work of three generations of women gardeners and was begun in the 1920's by Heather Muir. It is an intimate, personal garden with many secret delights and numerous rare shrubs hidden among its steep banks and corner. But its glory is its setting, and its roses. Kiftsgate is a dream of a garden.

And you can prolong the dream by walking the short distance to HIDCOTE MANOR GARDEN (Open daily April-Oct, except Tues & Fri,

11.00-6.00. Admission Charge. Tel: 01386-438333). The house is older here, a traditional Cotswold stone manor dating from the Tudor period, and owned by the National Trust. This is probably the most famous of all the Cotswolds gardens, the creation of an American, Major Lawrence Johnston who was a disciple of Vita Sackville West. It is hard to think of Hidcote as only one garden: it is a whole series of rather formal gardens, each more breathtaking than the last. Hidcote suffers from huge numbers of visitors so it is worth avoiding weekends and peak times.

We will loop back to Blockley now through the villages of Ebrington and Paxford and then retrace our steps down through Bourton-on-the-Hill to visit the last garden on our tour.

BATSFORD ARBORETUM (Open daily April-Nov, 10.00-5.00. Admission Charge. Tel: 01386-700409) is a garden created under the spell of the East. The first Lord Redesdale served as Ambassador to Japan in the 1850s and returned to the Cotswolds intent on reproducing its oriental beauty. He planted a fine Arboretum containing over 1000 named trees and you can buy many of these in the well stocked garden centre which is open all year round. Magnolias are the great speciality at Batsford – over 60 varieties are grown – but the maples and flowering cherries are also spectacular. Deer roam in the 50 acre parkland and you will be surprised by a collection of oriental statues dotted among the trees and shrubs. The other joy of Batsford is the FALCONRY CENTRE (Open daily, Mar-Nov, 10.30-5.30. Admission Charge. Tel: 01386-701043). There are flying displays throughout the day and you can watch a variety of eagles, falcons, hawks and owls being put through their paces.

## FURTHER EXPLORATION:

We have concentrated on grand gardens of the North Cotswolds in this tour but there is one other outstanding garden to be seen in the Cirencester area: Rosemary Verey's garden at BARNSLEY HOUSE (Open throughout the year, Mon, Wed, Thurs, & Sats only, 10.00-6.00. Admission Charge. Tel: 01285-740281). This famous garden has been an inspiration to countless gardeners. The laburnum walk is particularly beautiful in early summer, and Barnsley village itself is delightful.

Further south, near Tetbury, WESTONBIRT ARBORETUM has been mentioned already in TOUR 1 as another world-class gardening attraction.

On a smaller scale there is the PAINSWICK ROCOCCO GARDEN (see TOUR 9), the gardens of RODMARTON MANOR (see Tour 7), the formal gardens at SUDELEY CASTLE (see Tour 5) and the delightful gardens of CERNEY HOUSE, North Cerney (Open Feb-Oct. Tues, Wed & Fri only, 2.00-6.00. Admission Charge. Tel: 01285-831300).

Dozens of smaller private, but no less fascinating, gardens open to the public under the National Gardens Scheme each year, and these are all listed in their annual 'Gardens of Gloucestershire' leaflet (price 35p) obtainable from local tourist information centres and bookshops.

# 4. MERRILY, MERRILY, DOWN THE STREAM

Water is an integral feature of the Cotswold landscape, and each village grew up around its spring or stream. Water was an essential part of the early woollen trade which began on the high wolds of the north Cotswolds; and when the mechanisation of the industry demanded increasing supplies of water to power its mills, the industry moved southwards to the steep valleys around Stroud where the rivers are faster, deeper and more plentiful.

Water shaped the whole landscape with honey coloured cottages, stone churches and great barns clustering around the clear sparkling streams. And where there is water you will find willows and lush meadows, speckled trout and majestic herons. Water is probably the one element which gives the Cotswold countryside its distinctive timeless beauty.

Three of the rivers we follow in our tour, the Coln, Leach and Windrush, rise in the Cotswold hills and flow into the Thames. The Thames itself is a Cotswold river rising, from springs at Thameshead near Kemble. The fourth is the tiny river Eye which winds through the Slaughters.

This is an extensive tour starting at Bourton-on-the-Water taking in some of the most beautiful villages and countryside in England. Some of the villages are well known, others lie off the beaten track. But we will try to keep away from main roads and any sign of the twentieth century. Take a picnic, or break for lunch at a riverside pub. And why not buy some trout, or better still smoked trout, as a gastronomic souvenir?

# TOUR 4 – MERRILY, MERRILY
## DOWN THE STREAM

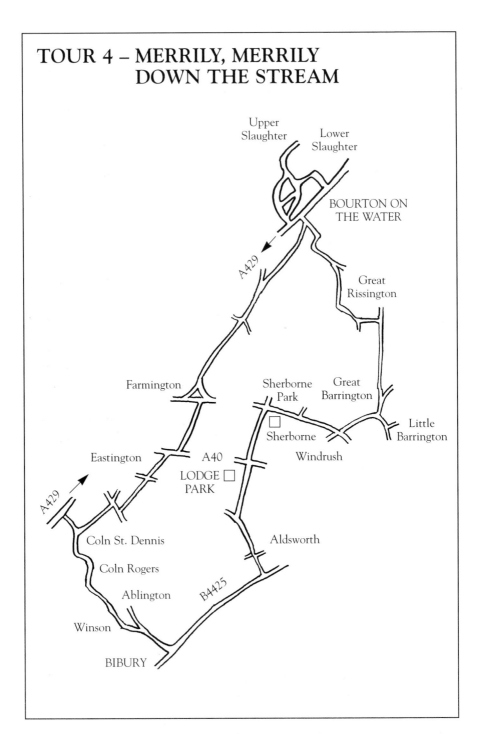

# DIRECTIONS:

From Bourton-on-the-Water turn right onto the A429 (direction Stow), but take the next turning to the left, just before the garage, to The Slaughters (1/2ml). First comes Lower Slaughter: cross the bridge and follow signs for Upper Slaughter. You can loop back to Bourton by a well sign-posted short circular route. Then follow signs through the village for The Rissingtons (The Barringtons and Burford) past the New Inn and Birdland.

After about 1ml turn right towards Great Rissington, and then left at The Lamb Inn to reach a T-junction with the Stow road (you will see Little Rissington airfield on the brow of the hill). Turn right onto this road, following the ridge until it drops down behind Barrington Park. Make a quick detour to Little Barrington – turn left at the red telephone box to find the church – and rejoin the road at the Fox Inn. Follow the river through Windrush and Sherborne, picking up signs, left, for Northleach and Oxford to take you to the busy A40. Go straight across the A40 and past the gates of Lodge Park.

Take the turning left to Aldsworth – the church spire is a mile away directly in front of you – and then turn right onto the B4425 towards Bibury (3mls). You will find the twisting road to Ablington immediately in front of the Swan Hotel. Turn left at Ablington and follow the Coln through Winson (1 1/2mls), Coln Rogers and Coln St. Dennis. From here you can either return to Bourton via the Fosse Way (A429) or stay off the main road by cutting over to Bourton via Eastington (N.B. this tiny road is signposted to Northleach), and across the A40 (signs to Farmington). Bourton is about 4mls over the downs from Farmington.

# APPROX. DISTANCE: 37 miles

# RECOMMENDED:

The Old New Inn, The Old Manse Hotel, Bo-Peep Tearooms, Rose Tree Restaurant at Bourton-on-the-Water; The Lamb Inn, Great Rissington; The Fox Inn, Great Barrington; Bibury Court Hotel, The Swan Inn, Javkowski's Brasserie, and The Catherine Wheel at Bibury.

*Bourton-on-the-Water.*

BOURTON-ON-THE-WATER likes to think of itself as the 'Venice of the Cotswolds'. The Windrush river runs sleepily through the town, crossed by a series of miniature stone bridges. There is an old-world feeling about Bourton that no amount of tourists and visitors can disturb. Everything is in harmony, the golden stone, the reflections of blossom trees in the water, the ducks, the sundials, the cottage gardens beside the water. And apart from its physical beauty, Bourton has its 'attractions' – a perfumery, a motor museum, a railway museum and a bird park. And if that isn't enough to lure visitors, it boasts a miniature replica of itself tucked away in the garden of the Old New Inn, a perfect stone MODEL VILLAGE (Open daily 9.00-6.00 summer, 10.00-5.00 winter. Admission Charge. Tel: 01451-820467) built to scale, where the tower of St. Lawrence's church reaches your waist and you must bend down to peep into cottage windows.

BIRDLAND (Open daily, Apr-Oct 10.00-6.00, Nov-Mar 10.00-4.00. Admission Charge. Tel: 01451-820480) is an oddity: a corner of the river Windrush that has become home to a large colony of penguins from the Falkland Islands and Antarctic as well as families of tropical macaws, parrots and graceful flamingoes which make the local ducks look rather staid and ordinary. The COTSWOLD PERFUMERY (Open Mon-Sat 9.30-5.30, Sun 10.30-5.30. Admission Charge. Tel: 01451-820698) is a family run business

*Lower Slaughter.*

producing perfumes and scented oils from over 600 ingredients. Linger in the small perfume garden and try the perfume quiz to see how your nose measures up. Or you could inspect the fascinating collection of vintage cars, toys and advertising signs at the COTSWOLD MOTOR MUSEUM (Open daily, Mar-Nov 10.00-6.00, Feb Sat & Sun only. Admission Charge. Tel: 01451-821255) or do some serious (miniature) train spotting at the BOURTON MODEL RAILWAY (Open daily Apr-Sept 11.00-5.00, Oct-Mar Sat & Sun only. Admission Charge. Tel: 01451-820686).

LOWER and UPPER SLAUGHTER must come a close second to Bourton-on-the-Water as the most photographed of the Cotswold villages and they lie so neatly together just the other side of the Fosse Way that it is worth making the short detour to include them in this tour. There are few "attractions" here other than the beech trees nodding over the sleepy river Eye, the glorious manor houses and modest cottages. If you are going to paint, this is the place to set up your easel.

You must go back into Bourton to pick up the road for the Barringtons as we shall go via Great Rissington, which is not on a river but has a splendid and ancient pub, the Lamb Inn. The airfield at Little Rissington at the top of the hill was home to the Central Flying School in the last war. The road along the top of the ridge leading down to the Windrush valley, skirts the massive walls of Barrington Park, a Palladian mansion designed by William Kent in 1738. You can just glimpse a fanciful 'temple' in the deer park through gaps in the high wall, but there is public access, up a small walled lane to the left of the main house gates, to GREAT BARRINGTON church, a rather austere little church with Norman origins and some fine 18th century monuments. LITTLE BARRINGTON church is another special place. It smells ancient and musty, but its treasures are its carvings: the tympanum above the main door of Christ and his angels, and the Elizabethan family figures on a tomb on the outside wall of the porch. The village, and its picturesque Post Office, is grouped around what was the quarry, now an uneven area of common land which in spring is covered in wild flowers.

WINDRUSH church has a fine Norman doorway with a double row of grotesque beakhead carvings and a collection of table tombs in the churchyard. The river meanders through the valley here and our road follows a particularly beautiful stretch into SHERBORNE. The National Trust owns the land around the great house here. Although the house itself has been converted into luxury flats, ample car parking is provided for walkers who want to follow clearly marked trails around the estate.

The land around Sherborne belonged to the Abbots of Winchcombe in medieval times when thousands of sheep grazed the lush pastures. The Dutton family rebuilt the house in the 17th century, and John Dutton succeeded in staying on good terms with both the Royalists and the Parliamentarians throughout the Civil War. A letter exists giving the authorization of Oliver Cromwell to stock Sherborne park with deer from nearby Wychwood Forest. Dutton was mad about hunting, and built a stylish lodge from which to view the chase. For many years LODGE PARK (just the other side of the A40) was thought to be the work of Inigo Jones. It is currently being restored by the National Trust and should be open to the public in 1996.

We cross over to another Cotswold river now, the Coln, and to do this we must drive through Aldsworth to BIBURY which was considered by William Morris to be the most beautiful village in the whole of England. The river seems alive with glistening irridescent trout; if you lean over the low stone walls you will see dozens of them, as well as a great variety of water fowl nesting on Rack Island where the weavers hung out their cloth to dry. Arlington Row, a line of tiny gabled weavers cottages, dates back to 1350. Henry Ford wanted to buy the whole thing – lock, stock and barrel – and take it back to America. He bought quite a few other Cotswold buildings, but luckily he failed to buy Arlington Row and the National Trust

*The Swan Hotel, Bibury.*

*Arlington Row, Bibury.*

bought it instead. You can buy your rainbow trout and other goodies at the BIBURY TROUT FARM (Open daily, Mon-Sat 9.00-6.00 - 5.00 in winter, Sun 10.00-5.00. Admission Charge. Tel: 01285-740215), a long established fishery in 8 acres right in the heart of the village. You can observe the whole process of fish-rearing, and even try your hand at catching your own supper. Failing this, trout are bound to be on the menu at the Swan Hotel or in the superbly situated Bibury Court Hotel in the manor house at the other end of the village.

*Ablington House.*

ABLINGTON'S claim to fame is that the manor here, built in 1590, was the home of J. Arthur Gibbs who wrote 'A Cotswold Village', the classic book which gives a fascinating insight into rural life in the last century. He chose one of the most beautiful spots on earth to make his home. You could leave the car and follow the Coln along the valley here. The villages follow one after another with barely a mile between them, but each has its own special atmosphere. The church of COLN ROGERS is Saxon, those at COLN ST. DENNIS and WINSON are Norman. You would not even have to move a television aerial to film a medieval street scene here, they seem quite untouched and perfect.

The Coln is crossed by the Fosse Way (A429) half a mile beyond Coln Rogers. If you are tired of winding roads you could go directly back to Bourton-on-the-Water on the Roman road at FOSSEBRIDGE. Otherwise, take the Northleach road on the left just behind the church at Coln Rogers which will take you through the hamlet of EASTINGTON on the Leach river, across the A40 to FARMINGTON and over the hill back into Bourton-on-the-Water.

## FURTHER EXPLORATION:

The rivers Leach and Coln join the Thames at LECHLADE. You can hire a boat here and row down the river (SEE TOUR 7).

Canal enthusiasts will find plenty to interest them on the STROUDWATER and THAMES AND SEVERN CANALS, stretches of which are being restored by the Cotswold Canals Trust (Tel: 01285-502797). The Trust runs summer weekend Boat Trips through the famous $2^{1}/_{2}$ml SAPPERTON TUNNEL.

The NATIONAL WATERWAYS MUSEUM at Gloucester (Open daily, winter 10.00-5.00, summer 10.00-6.00. Admission Charge. Tel: 01452-307009) is housed in an enormous Victorian warehouse on the docks and is well worth visiting.

*The Green, Farmington.*

# 5. THE AGE OF THE GOLDEN FLEECE

Sheep have dotted the landscape since man first settled the Cotswolds in Neolithic times. Sheep were eaten, milked, and their short coarse brown wool was woven into something warm to wear. The Romans introduced a superior, large, white breed with long curly wool, and before long, woollen cloth was actually being exported from the Cotswolds, hooded cloaks being particularly prized.

But it was the medieval wool trade which brought spectacular wealth to the region. Merchants arrived with their packhorses from France, Italy and Low Countries to haggle and trade in the lustrous heavy fleeces. Calais was still English and this was the age of the Golden Fleece. Fortunes were made, great churches were built on the proceeds, and most of the local population found employment in the wool trade in one way or another, either as spinners, weavers and dyers, or as simple shepherds. When William Tyndale wrote "God gave the earth to men to inhabit and not unto sheep", there were over half a million sheep on the Cotswolds.

Our tour begins in Northleach, a town founded in 1220 which owed everything to the fortunes of the wool trade. Its massive wealth paid for one of the finest churches in the Cotswolds and its subsequent decline ensured that the town remained untouched by the industrialization that changed the face of other wool towns like Stroud. Protected by a recent by-pass, Northleach is now a delightfully peaceful Cotswold town, and a perfect touring base for the North Cotswolds.

# TOUR 5 – GOLDEN FLEECE

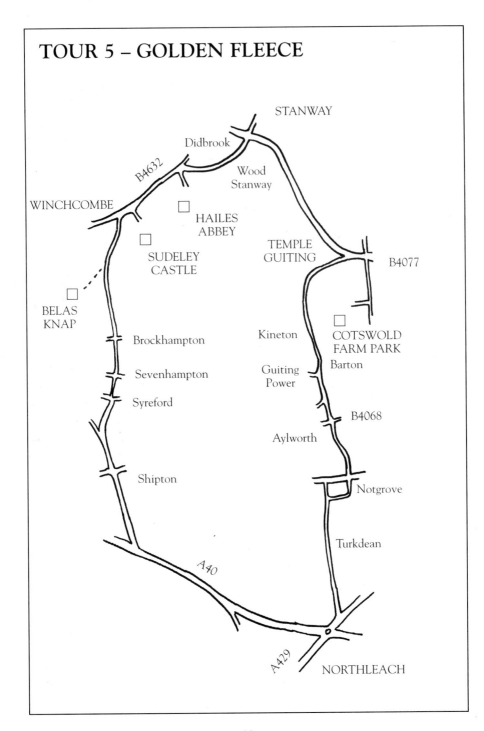

STANWAY

Didbrook

B4632

Wood
Stanway

WINCHCOMBE

HAILES
ABBEY

SUDELEY
CASTLE

TEMPLE
GUITING

B4077

BELAS
KNAP

Brockhampton

Kineton

COTSWOLD
FARM PARK

Barton

Sevenhampton

Guiting
Power

Syreford

B4068

Aylworth

Shipton

Notgrove

Turkdean

A40

A429

NORTHLEACH

# DIRECTIONS:

From Northleach take the A429 (Fosse Way) north towards Stow, and directly after the large roundabout with the A40 at the top of the hill, turn left for Turkdean and Notgrove. Turn right following the sign for Notgrove village, and left into the village proper. Just through the village you will arrive at a T-junction where you take the left turn marked Bourton-on-the-Water and Cheltenham. After 100 yards you will reach the A436 Cheltenham to Bourton road (Notgrove long barrow is just to the left here) and you cross this, dropping down through Aylworth. This twisting road takes you across the B4068, turn right at the junction and cross the Windrush river – Guiting Grange stud farm is on the right. Go on through Barton and Kineton to Temple Guiting where you can do a dog's leg through the village, right onto the B4077 and right again to reach the Cotswold Farm Park.

Go back onto the B4077 through Ford, and keep going down the steep escarpment as far as Stanway where you take the left turn marked Wood Stanway and Didbrook. Go under the railway bridge and turn left onto the main B4632 Cheltenham to Stratford road, and immediately left again to Hailes Abbey following the English Heritage signs (½ mile). Come back to this junction and turn left to go into Winchcombe. Sudeley Castle lies to the left of the town down Castle Street. Leaving Winchcombe on the B4632 (to Cheltenham) turn left just outside the town for Brockhampton – Belas Knap is 1½mls along here on the right, and a steep walk up the hill. Drive through Brockhampton, Sevenhampton, Syreford, across the A436, and down through Shipton to turn left onto the main A40 which will bring you quickly back to Northleach.

## APPROX. DISTANCE: 31 miles

## RECOMMENDED:

The Wheatsheaf Hotel, Wickens Restaurant, Red Lion Inn, Sherborne Arms, Corner Green Cafe, Northleach; Farmers Arms, Ye Olde Inne, Guiting Power; Cotswold Farm Park Cafe; Plough Inn, Ford; White Hart Inn, The Olde Bakery Tea Shoppe, Winchcombe; Craven Arms, Brockhampton; Puesdown Inn, Puesdown.

NORTHLEACH stands on the crossroads of the Fosse Way and the old coaching road from London to Gloucester. Since the A40 bypass was built Northleach has regained its peace and tranquility. Dominated by a massive wool church, the town square (for it is a proper town and not a village) is lined with specialist shops, old coaching inns, some half timbered and all welcoming, and there are two very good restaurants here.

The original houses were laid out by the Abbot of Gloucester on 'burgage plots', eighty of them measuring 20 rods by 2 rods (110 by 11 yards) and you can see this plan quite clearly from the playing fields across the river Leach. The weekly market was granted by charter in 1227, a date which is celebrated annually at the June Charter Fair. The ancient Court Leet still meets each November to elect the officers of the town, the High Bailiff, the Constable and the Sheriff, while children wait outside for the name of the new High Bailiff so that they can broadcast it around the town with the clanging and banging of pans.

The huge church, which now seems out of all proportion with the size of the town, was built with the proceeds of the wool trade. An enormously rich wool merchant John Fortey who died in 1458 rebuilt the earlier church on the site in the latest 15th century Perpendicular style. You will find his and his father's memorial brasses in the church. The collection of brasses at

*Northleach.*

Northleach, nearly all depicting wool merchants, is one of the finest in the country. Look for the details of a hedgehog, a snail, a pig and a crab nestling between the script exhorting us to "Pray for ye children of Thomas Fortey". Northleach has two fascinating museums. The COTSWOLD COUNTRYSIDE COLLECTION (Open daily Apr-Oct, weekdays 10.00-5.00, Sun 2.00-5.00. Admission Charge. Tel: 01451-860715) is instructive about the practicalities of the wool business and of farming and rural life in general. There is a splendid collection of haycarts, wagons and old farm implements as well as audio visual presentations about beekeeping, occasional demonstrations of country crafts, as well as a visit to the courthouse, for the museum occupies the old town prison. KEITH HARDING'S WORLD OF MECHANICAL MUSIC (Open daily 10.00-6.00. Admission Charge. Tel: 01451-860181) is housed in typical old wool merchant's house in Northleach High Street and has an amazing variety of musical boxes, automatic pianos, antique clocks, automata and mechanical musical instruments – all in noisy working order.

Leaving the old wool town we drive northwards onto the high wolds and sheep country. Before the Enclosures Act this was all open common land, and fairly desolate, according to Cobbett who rode through here on a Rural Ride in the 1820s. But now Cotswold farms are for millionaires, and you will pass some of the most enchanting country houses to be found in the whole country. These villages are particularly beautiful: TURKDEAN with its majestic avenue of beach trees and a tiny Norman church, NOTGROVE which belongs to one private estate but boasts a Saxon crucifix on the outside East wall of the church as well as monuments to members of Dick Whittington's family, and TEMPLE GUITING where the Knights Templar built a preceptory in the 12th century.

We are going to see sheep at close quarters now so turn off towards the COTSWOLD FARM PARK (Open daily end Mar-early Oct 10.30-5.00, July-Aug & summer Suns and Bank Hol Mons 10.30-6.00. Admission Charge. Tel: 01451-850307). There is always a high wind up here, after all we are at almost 800 feet up on the very top of the Cotswolds, but the views are breathtaking and this rare breeds survival trust is one of the most interesting attractions in the area. The original 'Cotswold Lion' sheep are gradually being reintroduced on the hills and this is where a number of them are bred. They are great big sheep with glamorous curls, and they positively dwarf the tiny Stone Age seaweed-eating Soay sheep from the island of St. Kilda. At lambing time the sheep are taken into the barn and you can watch the lambs being born; later in the year there are shearing and spinning demonstrations. The animals are straight out of

*Entrance, Stanway House.*

a children's picture book: cows with crumpled horns, Old Spot pigs, riotously decorated poultry, shire horses, and cheeky Angora goats.

You only realise how high you are in the Cotswolds when you actually look over the edge. Soon after the hamlet of Ford you reach the very top of the Cotswold escarpment. Winding down through the beech woods we pass STANWAY which has an exquisite 16th century manor house and tithe barn where occasional craft and antique fairs are held. STANWAY HOUSE (Open June, July & Aug. Tues & Thurs only 2.00-5.00. Admission Charge. Tel: 01386-584469), the home of Lord Neidpath, was used for location filming of Edith Wharton's 'The Buccaneers'.

From Stanway it is a short drive to Hailes Abbey at the foot of the escarpment. HAILES ABBEY (Easter to end Sept daily 10.00-6.00, Winter Tues-Sun 10.00-4.00. Admission Charge. Tel: 01242-602398) was one of the most important sites of medieval pilgrimage, for the Cistercian abbey contained a relic of the Holy Blood. Richard Earl of Cornwall, brother of King Henry III, built the abbey in gratitude for his life being spared after a terrifying shipwreck as he returned from the Crusade he led to the Holy Land in 1240. The magnificently endowed and wealthy abbey was destroyed at the Dissolution, but its remains are well preserved by English Heritage

and the National Trust who have built a small museum on the site. Your tour of the abbey ruins will be enriched by an audio-cassette guide which is included in the entrance charge.

WINCHCOMBE, which had its own abbey, is a fine historic Cotswold town in the heart of sheep country. In fact the Benedictine abbey owned one of the largest flocks of sheep in England. The great parish church with its grotesque gargoyles and the picturesque gabled houses and half timbered inns reflect the wealth of the area. The town is rich in royal associations. It was an important Saxon walled city in the Kingdom of Mercia, and the home of King Kenulf who founded Winchcombe abbey in 811. His son, later St. Kenelm about whose tomb many miraculous legends of healing grew up, was murdered at the age of seven. The destruction of the abbey in the Dissolution signalled the end of the town's prosperity, but the weekly market granted by the charter of Elizabeth I in 1575, and a flourishing trade in tobacco which lasted until Charles II put an end to it to protect the monopoly of the Virginia colonists, guaranteed the town's survival.

Catherine of Aragon reputedly embroidered the altar cloth in the town's church, you can see her symbol, the pomegranate, incorporated into the design.

*Sudeley Castle.*

*Carp pond and the ruins of Tithe Barn (c. 1440).*

Catherine of Aragon was also a visitor at nearby SUDELEY CASTLE (Open daily Apr-Oct, grounds 10.30-5.30, castle 11.00-5.00. Admission Charge. Tel: 01242-602308) as was Henry VIII, Anne Boleyn, Lady Jane Grey, Elizabeth I and Charles I. This romantic castle became the home of Henry VIII's last wife Katherine Parr. She remarried after Henry's death but died soon afterwards in childbirth and is buried in the castle chapel. The exquisite formal Queen's Garden is named after her. Sudeley has many art treasures and historic curiosities as well as an excellent garden centre and a children's adventure playground.

As you leave Winchcombe you will cross the tiny River Isbourne before climbing back onto the escarpment again on the road to Brockhampton – the views are particularly beautiful along here. After $1^{1}/_2$mls you will see the English Heritage sign for BELAS KNAP; pull the car in as well as you can on this narrow road and prepare for a stiff climb up through the woods (about $^3/_4$ml) to the top of the hill. It is well worth the effort, for apart from the view over the vale towards Wales there is a remarkably well preserved Stone Age long barrow dating from about 2500BC. The mound consists of a number of burial chambers protected by a false doorway to deter grave robbers. The tomb was excavated in 1863 and the remains of a young man of about 20 years old and five small children were found.

Our route back to Northleach takes us through the pretty villages of Brockhampton, Sevenhampton and Shipton – Shipton of course meant 'Sheep town'.

## FURTHER EXPLORATION:

COTSWOLD WOOLLEN WEAVERS (Mon-Sat 10.00-6.00, Sun 2.00-6.00. Admission Free. Tel: 01367-860491) at Filkins, just off the Burford to Lechdale road is a good example of a working Cotswold woollen mill. An extensive mill shop, exhibition area and coffee shop share the 18th century mill.

WOOLSTAPLERS HALL MUSEUM (Open daily Apr-Oct 11.00-6.00. Admission Charge. Tel: 01386-840289) at Chipping Campden offers the chance to see the interior of a 14th century wool merchants staple hall. The museum contains a collection of local memorabilia.

Rare breeds are the speciality of the COTSWOLD FARM PARK (see above) but you can also see a number of rare breeds of poultry and domestic waterfowl at FOLLY FARM WATERFOWL near Bourton-on-the-Water (Open daily 10.00-6.00 in summer, 10.00-3.30 in winter. Admission Charge. Tel: 01451-820285).

*15th century fan vaulting, Cirencester parish church.*

# 6. GOLDEN STONE

It is the quality and colour of the soft oolitic limestone which gives the Cotswolds its unifying beauty. Every cottage, barn and church in the region takes its warm golden colour from the easily carved and plentiful building material which has been worked here for thousands of years. Under a microscope the granules of stone look egg shaped, rather like a lump of fish roe, and thus the term 'oolitic' is a combination of the Greek words for 'egg' and 'stone'.

Today much of the new building is done with reconstituted Cotswold stone, but even this rarely offends the eye, since the most subtle variations of colour from one particular area or quarry are respected to provide an overall impression of harmony and continuity. Dozens of small quarries used to provide building material for the villages, a new quarry often being started right next to the church for which it was to provide stone. Shafts to disused mines are sometimes found under cellars in old village houses as the stone was mined in shafts up to half a mile long.

The abundance of easily carved stone brought a flowering in the mason's craft. We rarely know their names but merely catch a glimpse of an individual craftsman from his mason's mark scratched on a church pillar, or above a fireplace. Many of these masons were outstanding masters of their craft and when Sir Christopher Wren needed craftsmen to rebuild London after the Great Fire it was from the Cotswolds that he recruited his men.

The villages around Burford produced two famous families who worked for Wren in London, the Strongs and the Kempsters. But there have been many other such men, unknown masons from even earlier centuries, whose work on the churches and houses of these golden villages is their testimony.

# TOUR 6 – GOLDEN STONE

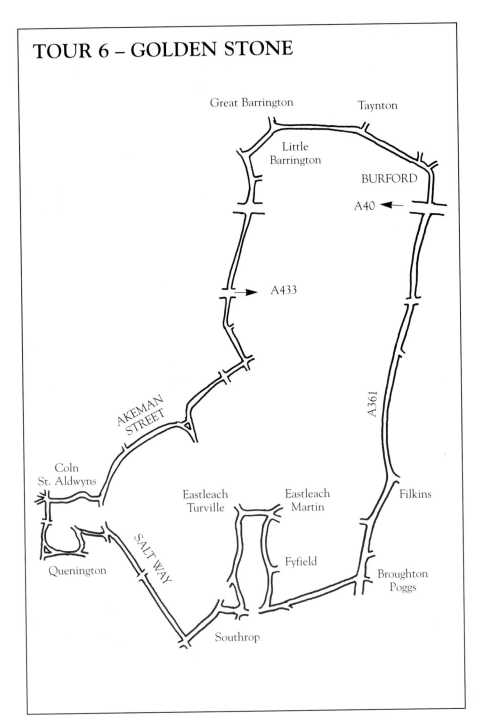

# DIRECTIONS:

Leave Burford northwards on the A429 turning immediately left to Taynton as you cross the Windrush. Follow the river through Taynton and Great Barrington, keeping left at the T-junction for Little Barrington. This road will bring you to the main A40 (Oxford to Cheltenham) road which you cross straight over. After 1ml you will cross the A433 (Burford to Aldsworth) road. Take the next turning right marked Eastleach Turville. The road descends steeply to the river Leach here and up the other side turn right towards Hatherop and Coln St. Aldwyn – this is the old Roman Akeman Street. At Hatherop turn right to Coln St. Aldwyns past Hatherop Castle School. At Coln St. Aldwyn the church is ahead of you up a No Through Road as you reach the village green.

From here it is barely $1/2$ml, across the river again, to Quenington. Go straight across the first cross roads at Quenington and left into the village at the large triangle. Pass two pubs on the left, and the Knights Templar gatehouse on the right before you come to the tiny church. You must turn round here before the river again and come back towards the pubs – turning right before them down Victoria Road. This tiny lane will lead you over a narrow stone bridge and onto the old Salt Road. Continue for 2 mls and turn left towards Southrop: the church is past the Swan Inn on the right. Return to the pub and turn right for Eastleach. Eastleach Turville is first, Eastleach Martin just across the stream. Keep straight on this road for about 2 mls to rejoin the main Lechlade to Burford A361.

# APPROX. DISTANCE: *22 miles*

# RECOMMENDED:

The Lamb Inn, The Bay Tree Hotel, The Golden Pheasant Hotel, Cotswold Gateway Hotel, Burford; The Fox Inn, The Inn for All Seasons, Great Barrington; The Swan Inn, Southrop; The Victoria Inn, Eastleach Turville.

The historic town of BURFORD lies just over the Oxfordshire border with Gloucestershire but is very much a Cotswold town with wonderful antique shops and pubs. Set on a steep hill, the main street rolls dramatically down to the Windrush river. Each house in this street is a work of art, and no two buildings are alike. Look at the quaint doorways, gables and roofs: 400 years separates some of them in style and form, but nevertheless the impression is one of absolute, well-weathered harmony. Give in to your curiosity and go inside the various shops and coaching inns, their interiors are entrancing. Imagine you are back in the seventeenth century with King Charles close by at Oxford and Oliver Cromwell rounding up the band of Levellers and imprisoning them in the town church. Charles and Nell Gwyn frequently stayed in the town during Bibury race week and their son later took the title Earl of Burford. In those days Wychwood Forest was full of deer and Burford was famed for its venison.

But you must imagine an earlier period still when you enter the parish church of St. John the Baptist past the quaint almshouses at the bottom of Church Lane: its origins are in the late 12th century. This church is more complex in plan than many Cotswold churches as a result of constant extension and rebuilding over a period of some 400 years. The wealth generated by the wool trade made Burford into one of the richest towns in

*High Street, Burford.*

the area. The town's guild of merchants dates from before 1100 and prosperity peaked around 1400.

Burford church was remodelled at this time, and the guild chapel which had stood apart from the church was incorporated into the building in 1422. There are many splendid tombs and monuments in the church and it is well worth buying the small guide book to help you identify them and understand the complex history of the building. Do not miss the strange pre-Christian stone, set high in the south wall of the turret, known as the 'Three Disgraces', or the pathetic

*Porch and Bale tombs, Burford Church.*

signature of one of the 350 imprisoned Levellers, a certain Anthony Sedley, who scratched his name on the rim of the font while awaiting execution in 1649. In the end Cromwell had only three of them shot and Anthony Sedley survived his ordeal.

Before you leave you must also seek out the elegant monument to Christopher Kempster on the wall of the south transept. Kempster, who lived to the ripe old age of 88 before retiring to 'Kit's Quarry', the house he built for himself on the edge of the town, was one of Wren's most famous master masons. His son William Kempster carved the fine monument with its weeping cherub which reminds us of his father's work on St. Paul's Cathedral and the city churches.

*Memorial to Christopher Kempster, Burford Church.*

Cross the narrow stone bridge over the river as you leave Burford and follow the winding Windrush along to TAYNTON. This village was the site of one of the most important local quarries in the 17th century and was used by Wren for St. Paul's and some of the Oxford colleges. It was also specified for the building of Blenheim Palace and repairs to Windsor Castle. The stone was taken on horse drawn wagons to the Thames at Radcot Bridge near Lechlade and transported by river downstream to London.

Taynton quarry (1½ml north of the village) was owned by Timothy Strong, another of the great Cotswold master masons. His son Valentine, who built Lower Slaughter Manor and probably Lodge Park at Sherborne, lived in a house in the village here known as 'Strong's House' with the date 1676 carved above the doorway. You can see his tomb in the graveyard at Fairford, where he died suddenly while building a great mansion at Fairford Park. Valentine had six sons, two of whom, Thomas and Edward (and Edward's son) worked for Wren. Thomas Strong laid the foundation stone of St. Paul's at a ceremony in 1675, and 33 years later, on Wren's 76th birthday in 1708 his brother Edward laid the final stone of the lantern on the dome. As you pass through the next village, Great Barrington, you will drive over 'Strong's Causeway' built in 1681 with money provided in the will of Thomas Strong 'to make a way between the Barrington bridges in Gloucestershire, that two men may goe a front to carry a corpse in safetie'.

GREAT BARRINGTON has a fine classical mansion, Barrington Park, the work of William Kent. And its adjacent church has two very good 18th century monuments, one by Joseph Nollekens to Mary, Countess Talbot (d.1787) and another depicting two children of the Bray family who died of smallpox being led over marble clouds by a winged angel. The entrance to the church is down a walled lane to the left of the main driveway.

We have touched on the Barrington villages before (SEE TOUR 4), but since this excursion is to provide a taste of the sheer vitality and scope of stone carving in the Cotswolds, we suggest that you return to these two villages to look more closely at the stone carving. LITTLE BARRINGTON has a wonderful 16th century monument and tomb on the outside wall of the church porch as well as an intricately carved Norman doorway and tympanum of Christ in Majesty surrounded by angels.

As you cross the main A40 and the landscape widens out, you will be aware of the sheer scale of Cotswold stone walling. Since the Enclosures Act dry stone walls have been built as field boundaries and stock enclosures running for thousands of miles over the hills. They were built to last for

*Typical Cotswold dry stone walling.*

centuries, but you may be lucky enough to spot a stone waller at work busy replacing the 'cocks and hens', a double row of upright stones, on the top of his wall, or arranging a single row of 'soldiers'. A three-man team can build 7 yards of walling in a day, but it is painstaking and expensive work, and thus a dying art.

Three villages nestle together in the Coln Valley, HATHEROP with its boarding school in the great house and its church with a broad French-style tower, COLN ST. ALDWYNS where there is more life – a shop and a pub as well as a pretty Norman church where John Keble's father was vicar for over fifty years, and idyllic QUENINGTON where the Knights Templar owned land in the 12th century. Their massive gateway stands beside the

road near the church, but it is the church of St. Swithin which we have come to see. It is one of the jewels of the Cotswolds: tiny, unassuming, yet adorned by two masterpieces of the late 12th century, its doorways.

Protected by a more modern porch, the sumptuously carved north doorway has a scene representing the Harrowing of Hell in which Christ triumphs over Sin, Death and the Devil, while its companion piece on the south side shows the Coronation of the Virgin, who holds a dove in her hand. Christ stands beside her while two angels stand guard above.

*North doorway, St. Swithin's Church, Quenington.*

Surrounded by their zigzag chevron mouldings, and supported by banks of twisting columns, these two carvings are among the finest of their kind in England. The interior of the church is simple and atmospheric and is at contrast with the richness and vitality of these early sculptures.

SOUTHROP church set by the manor house in the midst of a working farmyard, has another wonder, a font of the 12th century where the Virtues triumph over the Vices in eight small scenes. The Virtues, all men, subdue the Vices, all beasts. Their names are inscribed in Latin, those of the Vices being written backwards. There are also monuments in the church to the Keble family. John Keble, author of 'The Christian Year' and founder of the Oxford Movement, lived in the vicarage at Southrop and it was he who discovered the ancient font walled up in the south doorway.

As vicar of Southrop John Keble was also responsible for the two tiny churches in Eastleach, the last, and quite the prettiest, villages on our tour. A rickety stone clapper bridge across the Leach links the churches of Eastleach Martin and Eastleach Turville and is known to this day as 'Keble's Bridge'. There is a small pub here, daffodils by the river in spring, willows, ducks and ancient stones. Keble must have gazed at this beauty and reflected on the old saying "As sure as God's in Gloucestershire'.

*Norman font, Southrop Church.*

*Keble's Bridge, Eastleach.*

## FURTHER EXPLORATION:

The National Trust owns LODGE PARK, the elegant hunting lodge built by John Dutton at Sherborne and thought to be the work of Valentine Strong. It is due to reopen in 1996 after major refurbishment. (Tel: National Trust 01684-850051 for further information).

Vast quantities of reddish Taynton stone were used in the building of BLENHEIM PALACE (1704-1722) near Woodstock. (Open daily, 10.30-5.30. Admission Charge. Tel: 01993-811325). Documents survive relating to the difficulty experienced by the Strong family of masons who provided the stone and worked on the great palace in getting the Duke of Marlborough to pay his bills.

FARMINGTON STONE near Northleach (Tel: 01451-860280) is one of the most important working quarries in the Cotswolds. The advertisements for its sought-after natural stone fireplaces claim that Farmington stone was established 165 million years ago.

John Keble was born in KEBLE HOUSE at Fairford. Memorabilia from this house is now on display at ARLINGTON MILL MUSEUM at Bibury (Open daily, weekends only in winter. Admission Charge. Tel: 01285-740368).

# 7. ARTISTS AND CRAFTSMEN

It was almost entirely due to the influence of William Morris, writer, painter and craftsmen, that the Arts and Craft Movement came to the Cotswolds at the turn of the century. Years of continuing unemployment and poverty which followed the collapse of the woollen industry had forced workers to seek jobs in the factories of the Midlands, or emigrate; the Cotswolds were in deep, if picturesque, decline.

William Morris came across Kelmscott Manor in 1871 and, seeing at once the possibility of a revival built on local craftsmanship and tradition, wrote to his business partner: 'I have been looking about for a house for the wife and kids, and whither do you guess my eye is turned now? Kelmscott, a little village about two miles above Radcot Bridge – a heaven on earth; an old stone Elizabethan house . . . , and such a garden! close down by the river, a boathouse and all things handy.'

Kelmscott was to become a major source of Morris's inspiration, and a famous gathering place for artists, craftsmen and intellectuals. Even a hundred years after Morris's death, it remains a place of pilgrimage for admirers of the Arts and Craft Movement.

Fired by Morris's enthusiasm for Cotswold life, Ernest Gimson and Sidney and Ernest Barnsley moved to Sapperton in 1892. They set up cabinet making workshops in the village, creating handmade furniture for the arts and crafts revival that was now in full swing. Ten years later C. R. Ashbee brought his pioneering Guild of Handicrafts from London's East End to Chipping Campden. The Cotswolds are resonant with the influence of these men, the houses they built, the furniture they designed for them.

Make sure you choose a Wednesday for your Arts and Craft tour, since Kelmscott Manor is only open to the public on Wednesday afternoons in the summer. In the morning you could explore the Sapperton area, or drive over to Cheltenham where the town Art Gallery & Museum has a first class collection of Arts & Crafts furniture and silver. Lechlade on the infant river Thames is the perfect starting point for our tour.

# TOUR 7 – ARTISTS AND CRAFTSMEN

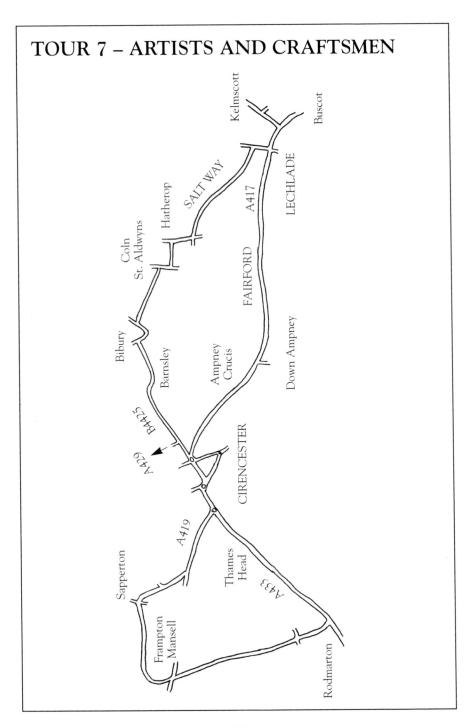

# DIRECTIONS:

After visiting the town, leave Lechlade on the A417 (towards Faringdon) but turn left onto the B4449 at St. John's Bridge for Kelmscott (2¹/₂mls). Retrace your steps back through Lechlade on the A417, but this time drive on through Fairford and Ampney Crucis to Cirencester. As you come into Cirencester you briefly join the A429. Go straight across at the 'Beeches' roundabout, and straight across at the first traffic lights (the town centre is next right from here).

For Sapperton we keep going here, through traffic lights, and right at the T-junction at the end of Querns Lane. Follow the one-way traffic left (the Cotswold Leisure Centre is on your right), and go right (for Stroud and Tetbury) at the roundabout in front of the hospital. Turn right at the next roundabout onto the A419 road to Stroud, but after 4mls turn right to Sapperton (1¹/₂mls).

Drive through the village leaving the church on your right; go straight across at the cross roads, and along the ridge through Frampton Mansell. Cross the A419 by the White Horse Inn, past the Cotswold Gliding Club at Aston Down. This road brings you through Rodmarton and down to the A433 Tetbury road, where you turn left for Cirencester. Follow directions for the Town Centre and come through the market place, back to the 'Beeches' roundabout. Go straight across on the A429 (Fosse Way), and keep going straight on (B4425) when the Fosse Way branches off to the left. Drive through Barnsley to Bibury where you take the right fork as you leave the village to Coln St. Aldwyns. Turn right as you come into the village; then turn left to Hatherop, and right again, bringing you onto the old Salt Way back down to Lechlade.

# APPROX. DISTANCE: 39 miles

# RECOMMENDED:

The Trout Inn, The New Inn, Lechlade; Kelmscott Inn, Kelmscott; The Bull Hotel, Hyperion House Hotel, Fairford; The Crown of Crucis, Ampney Crucis; Brewery Arts Coffee House, Harry Hare's Restaurant and Brasserie, The Fleece Hotel, The Kings Head, Cirencester; The Bell Inn, Sapperton; The Crown Hotel, Frampton Mansell; The Village Pub, Barnsley; Javkowski's Brasserie, The Swan Hotel, Bibury Court, Bibury; The New Inn, Coln St. Aldwyns.

*Riverside Boatyard, Lechlade.*

LECHLADE, standing at the point where the rivers Coln and Leach meet the Thames, seems straight out of 'The Wind in the Willows'. Hire a rowing boat at the Riverside Boatyard (Tel: 01367-252366) and set off with a picnic lunch to St. John's Lock to find the statue of Old Father Thames rescued from the ruins of Crystal Palace, or content yourself watching other people 'messing about in boats' from the peaceful garden of the old Trout Inn. There are delightful walks along the Thames here, and from wherever you are you can always see the graceful spire of Lechlade's wool church rising above the water meadows. The view inspired the poet Shelley to write his famous poem 'Summer Evening Churchyard' during his visit in 1815; a plaque on the church wall marks the beginning of 'Shelley's Walk'. Lechlade has a fine old church, a plethora of antique shops where you may be lucky enough to spot some authentic Arts and Crafts pieces, delightful pubs and picturesque gabled houses, all very much in the Cotswold tradition.

KELMSCOTT is a short drive from Lechlade (2¹/₂mls) but, on a fine day, you could follow the river path there on foot. William Morris was enchanted with the village and its Elizabethan house. He spent the last 25 years of his life here, and his body was brought for burial in the churchyard when he died in London in 1896. A simple gravestone designed by Philip

Webb marks the grave in the tiny churchyard, but there is a delightful image of the great man sitting under an apple tree, carved on a plaque on the Memorial Cottages.

KELMSCOTT HOUSE, owned by the Society of Antiquaries (Open Apr-Sept, Wednesday only, 11.00-1.00 & 2.00-5.00. Admission Charge. Tel: 01367-252486) is a shrine to William Morris, his wife Janie Burden and his friends, the painters Dante Gabriel Rossetti and Edward Burne-Jones. The house is a showcase for Morris's designs, the wallpaper, the fabrics, tapestries, the carpets, books from the Kelmscott Press, even the hangings for their four-poster bed. There are glorious pre-Raphaelite drawings and paintings of Janie and her children by Rossetti, who was a constant guest. Kelmscott was the destination of the narrator in Morris's 'News from Nowhere' (1891) and the subject of his essay 'Gossip About and Old House on the Upper Thames'.

While staying at Kelmscott Edward Burne-Jones worked on a series of paintings on the theme of 'The Sleeping Beauty' for the parlour of nearby National Trust-owned BUSCOT PARK (Open Apr-Sept, Wed, Thurs & Fri 2.00-6.00, also every 2nd & 4th Sat and Sun 2.00-6.00. Admission Charge. Tel: 01367-242094 not weekends), as well as on a series of stained glass windows for tiny Buscot church. The extraordinarily well preserved complete set of medieval glass at FAIRFORD was to provide Morris with the inspiration for his own first commission in stained glass for Selsey church, near Stroud, where he, Rossetti, Ford Madox Brown and Burne-Jones each designed a window.

We will pass through Fairford (SEE TOUR 8) and Cirencester (SEE TOUR 2) on our way to Sapperton. The Ampneys are pretty villages; DOWN AMPNEY (ALSO SEE TOUR 8) is best known for its association with the composer Vaughan Williams who was born at the Old Vicarage, and AMPNEY CRUCIS for its fine old church. CIRENCESTER has regular monthly (Saturday) Craft Markets at the Corn Hall (information from the Tourist Information Office), while a wide variety of local craftsmen are happy to accept your commissions, or show you their designs in the old converted Victorian Brewery Court Craft Centre in Cricklade Street (Tel: 01285-657181).

The village of Sapperton lies off the Cirencester to Stroud A419 road beyond the rather grand Royal Agricultural College, and land belonging to the Bathurst Estate which borders the left side of the road.

SAPPERTON, and the nearby houses at Daneway and Pinbury Park, formed the hub of the Arts and Craft movement in the Cotswolds in the early years of this century. Architects Ernest Gimson and two brothers,

*The Bell Inn, Sapperton.*

Sidney and Ernest Barnsley, first rented PINBURY PARK, a Tudor manor owned by the then Earl Bathurst on condition that they repaired it for him. (The gardens, but not the house, of Pinbury Park are occasionally open to the public through the National Gardens Scheme). As a young man Ernest Gimson had asked for William Morris's help in finding work with a London firm of architects (where the Barnsley brothers were articled), thus starting an enduring friendship based on the ideals of art and socialism. From Pinbury Park the craftsmen moved to another exquisite house, the ancient manor house at DANEWAY (visits by appointment only) where Earl Bathurst allowed them to set up workshops and showrooms for the handmade furniture they produced in conjunction with local craftsmen.

Sapperton church has a fine setting overlooking the golden Frome Valley and the graves of the three craftsmen lie side by side in the churchyard. But their memorial lies all around them in the cottages and houses they built in the village: Upper Dorvel House was Ernest Barnsley's house, Sidney lived at Beechanger and Ernest Gimson built The Leasowes. From the garden of the Bell Inn you can observe the almost miniature Village Hall, built by Ernest Barnsley in 1912, where Mrs Gimson organised Morris dancing and Cecil Sharpe came down to judge folk singing festivals and the extravagant (and competitive) topiary in the cottage gardens. Norman Jewson, who lived at Batchelor's Court and married Ernest Barnsley's daughter Mary, was a particular devotee of topiary, peacocks being his speciality.

The road between Sapperton and Frampton Mansell has spectacular views across the Frome Valley. The little Alpine-style church at Frampton Mansell, built by the 4th Earl Bathurst in 1844 and inspired by his Grand Tour, hardly looks out of place on the steeply wooded hillside.

Between 1909 and 1926 Ernest Barnsley cycled along this road to RODMARTON engaged on his most important project, the building of one of the last manor houses to be built in Britain. Commissioned by banker Claud Biddulph, the great five bay house was to be built entirely out of stone quarried on the estate, wood cut from estate timber, while much of the actual construction work was carried out by estate workers. Most of the furniture for the house and chapel was made locally by members of the Arts and Craft Movement. When Ernest Barnsley died, his brother Sidney briefly took over the work, the 20 year project eventually being completed by Norman Jewson. The gardens designed by Mary Biddulph at Rodmarton are particularly beautiful, and well worth visiting, although the house itself is not open to the public (Gardens and chapel open Sat only 2.00-5.00, mid May-end Aug. Admission Charge. Tel: 01285-841253).

From Rodmarton we return to Cirencester on the Tetbury road, passing very close to the source of the river Thames by the railway bridge at Thames Head. We take a very pretty route back to Lechlade passing through the village of BARNSLEY where the world famous gardener designer and author Rosemary Verey lives at Barnsley House (gardens open Mon, Wed, Thurs & Sat 10.00-6.00. Admission Charge. Tel: 01285-740281). (SEE TOUR 3).

Our final destination is the village of BIBURY described by William Morris as 'the prettiest village in England'. An interesting collection of material relating to the Arts and Craft Movement can be seen in a 300 year old corn mill on the river Coln. ARLINGTON MILL MUSEUM (Open daily, weekends only in winter. Admission Charge. Tel: 01285-740368) has, among other curiosities, a room devoted to William Morris (and another to John Keble, SEE TOUR 6) as well as a collection of furniture made by members of the movement.

From Bibury it is a pretty drive through Coln St. Aldwyns and neighbouring Quenington (ALSO SEE TOUR 6) onto the straight old Salt Road which brings us back down into Lechlade.

## FURTHER EXPLORATION:

CHELTENHAM ART GALLERY AND MUSEUM in Clarence Street has a collection of Arts & Craft furniture and silver (Open Mon-Sat 10.00-5.20. Closed Bank Hols & Suns. Admission Free. Tel: 01242-237431).

Two churches with important Arts & Crafts associations are at SELSEY and CHALFORD, both in the Stroud area.

BROADWAY TOWER, a Gothic folly overlooking the Cotswold escarpment near Broadway, where Morris, Rossetti and Burne-Jones were frequent visitors, has a William Morris exhibition (Open daily Apr-Oct 10.00-6.00. Admission Charge. Tel: 01386-852390).

CHIPPING CAMPDEN retains a strong arts and craft tradition. Of particular interest is the Robert Welch Studio Shop in the Lower High Street. Tel: 01386-840522, a showcase for pioneering design in silver and stainless steel.

Pottery enthusiasts will find plenty to interest them in the Cotswolds. The well known WINCHCOMBE POTTERY just outside the town (Open Mon-Sat & summer Sundays. Tel: 01242-602462) has a range of craft workshops including a goldsmith, sculptor and furniture maker.

Distinctive pottery is also made by the Benedictine monks of PRINKNASH ABBEY near Painswick (Open daily. Pottery tours Mon-Sat 10.30-4.00 & Sun afternoons. Closed for lunch 12.30-1.30. Shop open 9.00-5.00. Abbey Church open 5.00a.m-09.00p.m. Admission Charge. Tel: 01452-812239).

# 8. BIRDS, BEASTS AND MYTHICAL CREATURES

Driving along the quiet country roads you might catch the flash of a fox's tail in your headlights or spot the nervous shadow of a fallow deer standing in the trees; you will certainly see enough pheasants to wonder why there is any sport in shooting them. There are countless birds and beasts in the wooded valleys of the Cotswolds; and if you look carefully, many of the churches are adorned with their images.

This tour aims to explore the wealth of flora and fauna of the Cotswolds from the waders and dippers of the man-made lakes and the delicate wild flowers of the water meadows, to the purple serpent in the Garden of Eden and 'Tiddles' the church cat.

Bring binoculars, if you have them, for bird and aircraft spotting. They are also invaluable for looking at architectural details, and especially at stained glass. Wellington boots might be useful and, if you are unsure of the difference between a pochard and a widgeon, bring a bird book to help you identify some of the unfamiliar species in the nature reserves. Lastly, try and obtain a copy of the Cotswold Water Park leaflet which gives an excellent sketch map showing the lakes and facilities: you should find one at any of the local tourist information centres.

Follow the Countryside Code and keep your eyes open for all kinds of wildlife: there are encouraging signs of otters reappearing in the Cotswold rivers, and crayfish lurk in the streams as well as trout. Who knows what you may see?

# TOUR 8 – BIRDS, BEASTS AND MYTHICAL CREATURES

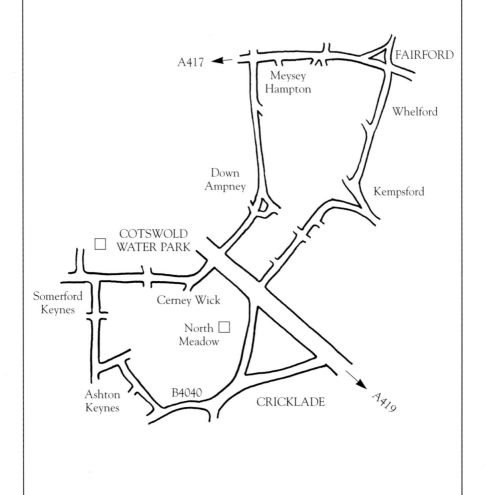

# DIRECTIONS:

Leave Fairford on the A417 road (to Lechlade) and, just before the filling station, take the first right to Whelford. Go through the village, skirting RAF Fairford, and on to Kempsford. The church is signposted to the right. From Kempsford keep on going, past the turning to Meysey Hampton, until you reach the busy A419 road to Swindon and the M4. Turn left onto the dual carriageway, but take the very next exit off it again into Cricklade town. This approach road brings you to a T-junction in the town centre, turn right and keep going as if you were going to rejoin the A419 but in the opposite direction. On the left, just before the main road, you will see signs to the North Meadow Nature Reserve.

After visiting the reserve, go back into Cricklade, past the town clock and turn first right onto the B4040 to Ashton Keynes. After 1ml turn right again and drive through Ashton Keynes, past the church, and turn left at the next crossroads. You will see the signs for the Cotswold Water Park almost immediately, on the right. Come back to this junction again, turn left and continue to the A419. Go right across the main road towards Down Ampney, through Meysey Hampton, and back to Fairford on the A417.

# APPROX. DISTANCE: 31 miles

# RECOMMENDED:

The Bull, Fairford; The Axe & Compass, Kempsford; The Plough Inn, Ashton Keynes; The Masons Arms, Meysey Hampton.

People come from all over the world to see the complete set of medieval stained glass of FAIRFORD which is almost unique in Europe. The 15th century church of St. Mary's stands at one end of the market place, a massive building dominating the town, and evidence of the enormous wealth of the Cotswold wool trade. The brasses and tombs of the wool merchant who built this church, John Tame, and his wife Alice, who died in 1471, as well as their son Edmund who completed the church, bring a human dimension to the great building. They lie in a strangely foreign landscape (the master glazier Bernard Flowers was Flemish) surrounded by a cast of thousands: biblical characters, mythical beasts, historical figures, heavenly angels, terrifying demons and a panoply of brightly coloured birds and beasts, all of whom come dazzlingly to life as the sun shines through the coloured window panes. From the main door cross to the North side of the

nave and find the window showing Adam and Eve deep in conversation with the purple serpent in the Garden of Eden. This is the starting point for reading the series rather as you would a strip cartoon. The official short guidebook to the stained glass is highly recommended.

As for birds and beasts (we will not include the 69 carved angels that have been counted in the roof alone), they are everywhere you look. Especially beautiful are the carvings on the undersides of the choirstalls, or 'misericords', where you will see a variety of animals and birds in charming country scenes: two old women plucking a fat pigeon, a fox snarling at geese, a hawk attacking a

*Grave to" Tiddles" the church cat, Fairford Church.*

68

duck, and a couple of ill-assorted country dogs. Outside the church, on the tower and roof you will see some particularly splendid grotesques and gargoyles as well as representations of local animals like the Cotswold sheep and the rabbit. Can you see the little old stone man trying to climb off the church roof? The stone monument to 'Tiddles' the church cat sit beside the porch gate, and people with long, fond memories still put flowers on his grave.

Between Fairford and Lechlade there are a number of flooded gravel pits which form part of the COTSWOLD WATER PARK. As we leave Fairford we will catch sight of the first of these just after the turning to Whelford. All the lakes are numbered: the first one we pass on the right is Lake 105, home of the COTSWOLD MOTOR BOAT RACING CLUB (Tel: 01285-712893). You could pull in here for coffee and book a lesson at the WATER SKI CLUB (Tel: 01285-713735). There are over 100 lakes in the park, 80 of them further south in the Ashton Keynes area which we will explore later in this tour. Every kind of water sport is catered for, from windsurfing and jet skiis to sailing and canoeing. Facilities for coarse and game fishing at the many lakeside clubs are excellent.

WHELFORD, standing in the shadow of the huge airbase of RAF FAIRFORD, is very much a farming village. The road through the village passes within yards of the end of the main runway and provides a fantastic view of the base and its comings and goings. Concorde was tested here in the 1970s much to the dismay of Fairford residents fearful that vibration might damage the stained glass. During the Gulf War American B52 bombers shook the sky as they took off on their bombing missions to Iraq.

The next village, another small place but with a very large church, is KEMPSFORD. The 15th century Perpendicular church with its eyecatching interior decoration is well worth a visit. There is good Victorian glass here, and an ornate ceiling featuring no less than 16 blood red Tudor roses. An explanation of the origins of the Tudor rose hangs on the wall near the door. The *Rosa gallilica officinalis*, brought back to England by the Crusaders in the 12th and 13th centuries, was prized for its medicinal properties. This rose became the emblem of the House of Lancaster while the House of York adopted its white version. At the end of the 'Wars of the Roses', the two emblems were fused into one 'Tudor Rose'. You can see a real 'apothecary's rose' planted in the flower bed by the church door.

The Wiltshire countryside is extremely flat here and the tower of St. Sampson's in Cricklade is visible for miles around. To reach Cricklade we must briefly cut onto the extremely busy A419 road to Swindon and the M4 but almost immediately turn off again into the town. CRICKLADE is a

*Snakeshead Fritillary, North Meadow Nature Reserve, Cricklade.*

historic Saxon town with a fine, early church where an annual music festival is held. The church is sometimes locked but a key can be obtained from the vicarage.

But Cricklade is not really a Cotswold town in the true sense; what interests us here is the NORTH MEADOW NATURE RESERVE where in late April and May the ancient water meadow is carpeted with the strangely-spotted snakeshead fritillary. Other wild flowers bloom in abundance: oxeye daisies, buttercups, great burnet and cuckoo flowers. The towns people of Cricklade have had the right to graze their animals on this meadow after the hay is cut for hundreds of years. and they still do so, but you may walk around the nature reserve guided by information boards which point you in the right direction. (Information from the Site Manager, Tel: 01380-726344).

The main part of the COTSWOLD WATER PARK lies in the area around Ashton Keynes and there is quite a lot of traffic on the narrow roads to and from gravel pits which are still being worked. It is surprising how quickly wildlife takes over when extraction stops. Sandmartins, ringed plovers, terns and waders actually prefer the barer gravel sites. KEYNES COUNTRY PARK (Park open daily 9.00-9.00. Beach open daily 1.00-5.00 weather permitting. Car park charge. Tel: 01285-861459) is a well established nature reserve and leisure area situated on Lakes 31, 32 and 34. An extremely well-organised Rangers Office will supply you with leaflets of suggested walks you may take, and provide expert information on what to see and where to see it.

A record book in the bird-watching hide on Lake 34 will tell you what has been spotted most recently. This lake is particularly interesting as a summer breeding place and has large colonies of red crested pochards and great crested grebe. It is also the place to see hobbies attracted by great clouds of dragon flies and damsel flies in the early summer. The larger lakes on the other side of the road (Lakes 31 and 32) have seven species in nationally important numbers: the Mute swan, gadwall, pochard, great crested grebe, tufted duck, coot, and Canada goose. The aquatic vegetation in the lakes is also important, ten of the Water Park lakes being designated Sites of Specific Scientific Interest.

The wildlife of the area is portrayed in a touching tribute to two young local people who died in the Herald of Free Enterprise disaster at Zeebrugge. A large, exquisitely-engraved glass screen in the church at ASHTON KEYNES depicts dragon flies, herons, grebes, the fritillaries – in fact all the birds and wild flowers that we will have seen on our tour.

Our final stop on this tour is at DOWN AMPNEY back on the other side of the A419. Ralph Vaughan Williams, who was born at the Old Vicarage on 12th October 1872, immortalised his birthplace in the famous hymn tune which bears its name. This tiny church honours the great English composer with a small display of memorabilia. It also has a peculiar decorative scheme, a pattern of tiny red flowers painted all over the arches and ceilings which date from the 14th century: they are said to be a reminder of the Black Death which devastated the village. The survivors burned all the houses, and when they rebuilt them on another site, the old church had become isolated from the village. It is difficult to say what type of flowers they represent, but it seems

*Down Ampney churchyard.*

they are the roses referred to in the children's nursery rhyme 'Ring a Ring of Roses'. A rosy rash encircled the helpless victim, he started sneezing, and soon he fell down dead. Today the little roses just seem charming: perhaps they have nothing to do with plague at all.

## FURTHER EXPLORATION:

Near Gloucester, the 250 acre ROBINSWOOD HILL COUNTRY PARK run by the Gloucestershire Wildlife Trust (Tel: 01452-383333) promotes wildlife conservation. It is a place for all the family, with scenic woodland trails, picnic areas, and exciting interactive displays in the new visitor centre.

Right up on the top of the Cotswold escarpment with marked trails and a visitor centre, is CRICKLEY HILL COUNTRY PARK (Open daily. Admission free. Tel: 01452-863170). This interesting park has superb views over the vale towards Wales and is a site of particular archaeological importance.

A leaflet on COTSWOLD AND GLOUCESTERSHIRE FARM ATTRACTIONS available from tourist information centres lists 15 places, ranging from a vineyard to a collection of rare domestic waterfowl.

# 9. LITERARY TOUR

The Cotswolds have long attracted poets and writers. A succession of writers from Daniel Defoe to Nancy Mitford, not to mention the important school of poets which flowered in and around Dymock before the First World War, have either passed through or settled in this picturesque part of England. Some people even think that William Shakespeare spent his 'lost years' in the Dursley area before bursting onto the London stage, since his Cotswold references have an insider's accuracy.

Today one's own preconceived ideas of life in Gloucestershire are likely to be the result of reading the popular novels of Jilly Cooper or Joanna Trolloppe, both of whom live in the Stroud area. In the same way previous generations discovered the Cotswolds through the pages of Laurie Lee's memorable autobiography *Cider with Rosie*.

In literary terms our tour covers a great deal of ground, from ancient to modern, sacred to profane. We start in Painswick and explore the Stroud area chosen by many successful, contemporary writers for its breathtaking views and the privacy of its deep secluded valleys. It takes as its southernmost point, on the very edge of the Cotswolds, the monument to William Tyndale, translator of the Bible into English, and arguably the single most important influence on our language and literature.

# TOUR 9 – LITERARY TOUR

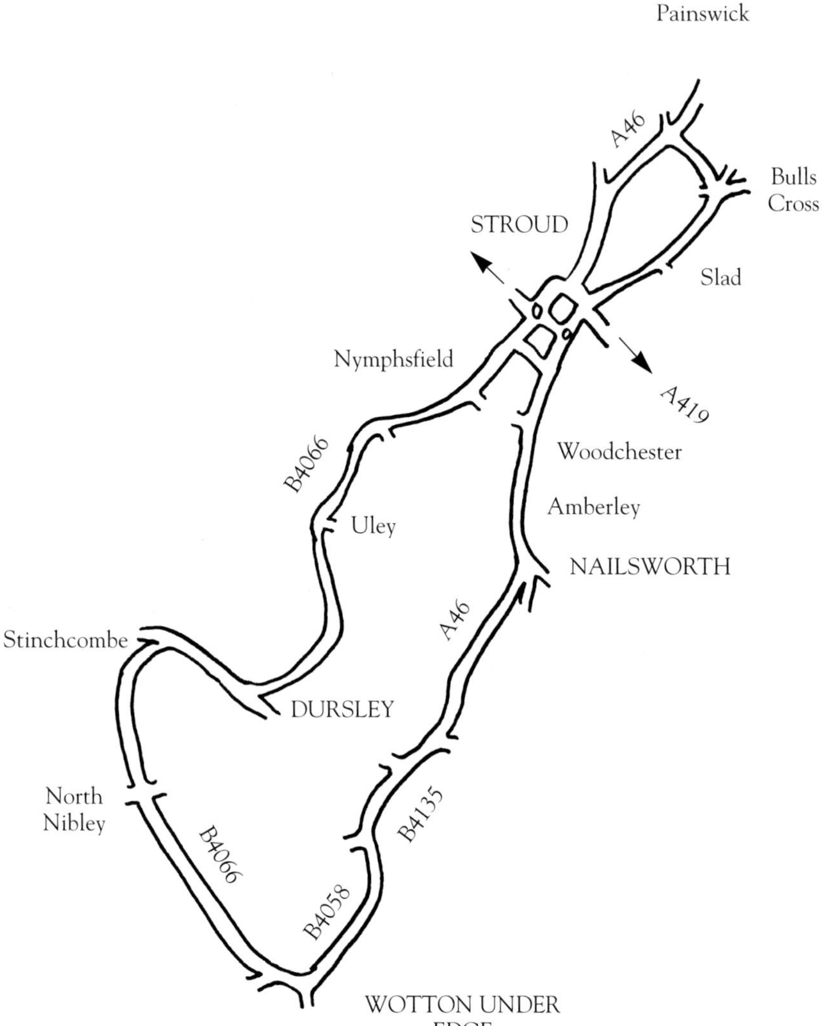

Painswick

A46

Bulls
Cross

STROUD

Slad

Nymphsfield

A419

B4066

Woodchester

Amberley

Uley

NAILSWORTH

A46

Stinchcombe

DURSLEY

North
Nibley

B4066

B4135

B4058

WOTTON UNDER
EDGE

# DIRECTIONS:

Painswick lies 3mls north of Stroud on the A46 road (to Cheltenham). At the crossroads in the main street, beyond the church, there is a signpost pointing right to Slad (2mls). Take care on this stretch of road as it is very steep, narrow and winding. From Slad we drive down into Stroud on the B4070 and turn right at the roundabout following signs to the A419. We pick up the Scenic Route B4066 (direction Dursley) at the next roundabout. This takes us along the high Cotswold ridge, through Uley and into Dursley. Go right through the town, following signs for Gloucester. At the modern police station just outside town turn left onto the B4060 to Stinchcombe. This road takes us past the North Nibley monument to Wotton-under-Edge. At Wotton we cut back to Nailsworth on the B4058 where we rejoin the busy A46 for a short drive back into Stroud.

# APPROX. DISTANCE: 39 miles

# RECOMMENDED:

The Falcon Inn, The Country Elephant Restaurant, St. Michael's Restaurant, Painswick Hotel, Painswick; The Woolpack, Slad; Mills Cafe, Stroud; Owlpen Manor Restaurant, Old Crown Inn, Uley; Black Horse Inn, North Nibley; Tubby's, Nailsworth.

PAINSWICK stands on the crown of a very steep hill, and it seems more of a town than a village. Nevertheless it remains one of the loveliest places in the Cotswolds. Prosperity came late to Painswick, in the 17th and 18th centuries. Fortunes were made – and subsequently lost in the depression which followed – in the cloth and dyeing trade which had moved from the North Cotswolds to the Stroud area, attracted by the plentiful water supply for the great woollen mills. Most of the important houses in Painswick's main street are Georgian, as indeed are the grander houses of the outlying villages, and the village has an elegance as well as a charm that is quite unmatched. The 6 acre restored 18th century PAINSWICK ROCOCO GARDEN (Open mid-Jan-end Nov, Wed-Sun & Bank Hol Mons, 11.00-5.00. Admission Charge. Tel: 01452-813204) just outside the village illustrates this elegance well.

Stroud was famous for its scarlet cloth, which was fashioned into military uniforms for Wellington's troops at the Battle of Waterloo. Nearby Uley produced high quality blue cloth, and today the green baize for billiard tables is still produced in the area.

Painswick churchyard is one of the great sights of the Cotswolds. 99, or possibly 100, yew trees, all clipped like living sculptures, form geometric

*Painswick.*

*Ancient yews and tabletop tombs, Painswick churchyard.*

lines between the famous 'tabletop' tombs. They say 99 trees were planted, but the Devil always takes the 100th no matter how many times it is planted. But the yews are almost impossible to count, for they are so twisted and gnarled and grown into each other that there might be half that number of perhaps twice as many. In September each year there is the famous ceremony of 'clipping' the yews, when the villagers encircle the ancient trees holding hands in a human chain.

As a child Laurie Lee stared across at Painswick sprawling 'white in the other valley, like the skeleton of a foundered mammoth'. SLAD is a mere two miles from Painswick, but, up and down precipitous hillsides, and past Bulls Cross, it must have seemed another world away. The poet was three years old when his mother and his seven brothers and sisters moved to a picturesque but tumbledown cottage in the tiny village of Slad. His childhood reminiscences of Cotswold life in the 1920s in the bewitching 'Cider with Rosie' have delighted generations of readers. Laurie Lee still lives in Slad and can sometimes be found in the 'Cider with Rosie' bar at the Woolpack. The cottage where he grew up has changed hands, and names. 'Rosebank' nestles in the hillside below the main road, on the bend above the Woolpack.

There is a wonderful description in the book of the charabanc on the Annual Slad Choir Outing thundering down the hill from Slad to Stroud.

*Iron-Age burial mound, Nymphsfield.*

We take this road into busy, industrial Stroud but escape back up onto the height of the Cotswold escarpment following the Scenic Route (B4066) to Dursley. Just off this road beyond Stroud is Woodchester, site of the famous Roman mosaic pavement which lies buried under the churchyard. If you cannot actually see the 'Great Orpheus Pavement', you can visit the romantic unfinished ruins of WOODCHESTER HOUSE (Open Sat/Sun 1st weekend in every month, and Sat/Sun/Mon on Bank Hol Weekends, 11.00-4.00. Admission Charge. Tel: 01453-860531).

The Cotswolds have a different character here after the closely-wooded, almost Alpine valleys above Stroud. You feel you are on top of the world up on this great windswept ridge; the dramatic views extend across the snaking, silvery river Severn to Wales. It is easy to understand why this magnificent site was chosen by the Stone Age builders of HETTY PEGLER'S TUMP, just a short walk across fields from the road. If you have a torch, and are feeling brave, you can crawl inside the 5,000 year old long barrow – 15 skeletons were found inside when the burial chamber was excavated in 1854.

The road continues with spectacular views through ULEY, which has an impressive Iron Age hillfort and an exquisite Tudor Manor House (OWLPEN MANOR, ULEY, Open Apr-Sept, 2.00-5.00, Tues, Thurs, Sun

& Bank Hol Mons, and Weds July-Aug. Tel: 01453-860261). We are close to the Severn now and Berkeley Castle is within striking distance.

STINCHCOMBE or 'Stinkers' as Evelyn Waugh nicknamed it is barely a mile from Dursley and has a fine golf course. After his marriage to Laura Herbert in 1937 Waugh settled at Piers Court to finish his comic masterpiece *Scoop*. The imposing Georgian mansion is not open to the public, but its stone gate pillars are visible just beyond the lane leading to the village. Waugh lived here for nearly 20 years producing some of his finest work, including *Brideshead Revisited* and *The Loved One*.

Soon after Stinchcombe you will see the great monument at NORTH NIBLEY, built in 1866 to commemorate the birth of William Tyndale in 1484. A signpost points the way up from the road, but if you intend to climb the 111ft high tower with its extensive views over the Severn estuary, you must first obtain the key (Tel: 01453-542357 for further information, or ask at the delightful Black Horse pub in the village, they will know who has it). Tyndale, who translated the New Testament from Latin to English so that it could be read and understood by every man, woman and child in the land, was hounded into exile in Flanders, arrested on the orders of Henry VIII and executed at Vilvorde in 1536. Despite the grandeur of this memorial, North Nibley reluctantly shares its claim to fame as Tyndale's birthplace with a number of other villages in the area including Slimbridge and Cam.

*The monument to William Tyndale, North Nibley.*

WOTTON-UNDER-EDGE is a town on the very edge of the Cotswolds as its name implies. Proud of its past, the town has opened a small Heritage Centre in the old Fire Station (Open Tues-Sat 10.00-5.00 Summer, and 10.00-4.00 Winter. Admission Charge. Tel: 01453-521541) where you can learn something of its history, trace any family connections you may have in the reference room and take advice on further exploration of the area. On a literary note, Isaac Pitman, the inventor of shorthand, was a schoolmaster in the town. A plaque on a house in Orchard Street commemorates his stay in Wotton.

The road back to Stroud rises steeply again from Wotton affording magnificent views from the top of the ridge. We drive on through hilly Nailsworth where the local landmark is the Nailsworth Ladder, an incredibly steep hill said to have a gradient of nearly one in two.

Readers of *John Halifax, Gentleman* may recognise corners of AMBERLEY from Mrs Craik's descriptions of 'Enderley'. Although the novel is primarily set in Tewkesbury, the author stayed for a while in Amberley in the mid 1850's at Rose Cottage.

Beatrix Potter makes several references to Stroud in her letters. She was staying with her cousin at nearby HARESCOMBE GRANGE when she first heard the charming story that led to the creation of 'The Tailor of Gloucester' which was published in 1904.

The valleys around Stroud provide settings to several of the best-selling novels of Jilly Cooper, who lives at Bisley. Her witty descriptions of life in the exotic polo-playing, show-jumping Cotswolds seem a long way from Laurie Lee's poetic reminiscences of rural life before the age of television and the motor car.

## FURTHER EXPLORATION:

Beatrix Potter fans, young and old, will love THE HOUSE OF THE TAILOR OF GLOUCESTER tucked away in College Court behind Gloucester Cathedral (Open weekdays 9.30-5.30. Admission Free. Tel: 01452-422856). Straight out of the bewitching illustrations for the children's tale, the little house displays a collection of memorabilia and sells all kinds of Beatrix Potter merchandise.

CHELTENHAM hosts a world famous LITERARY FESTIVAL in October each year with leading writers and personalities addressing audiences in a packed two week programme with fringe events. (Information from Festival Box Office, Town Hall, Imperial Square, Cheltenham. Tel: 01242-227979).

# 10. COLOURFUL CHARACTERS

The Cotswolds seem to have had their fair share of eccentrics and we are fortunate that posterity has preserved some of their wilder excesses. It seems perhaps unfair to credit the area around Chipping Campden with the highest proportion of eccentricity, but on this tour we will meet a number of personalities who left their mark on both the Cotswold landscape and on the history of England.

In addition to obsessive collectors, sporting promoters and indulgent earls, we will find traces of painters, scholars and courtiers who either lived 'under the edge' or on top of the edge. Our tour takes us south west from historic Chipping Campden, along the 'spring line' villages to Broadway at the base of the great escarpment, up through Snowshill, and returning to 'Chippy' (to give it its local nickname) along the top of the ridge.

We will be passing through some beautiful scenery and several of the prettiest villages in the Cotswolds. We briefly stopped at Chipping Campden on our 'Garden' tour (TOUR 3), but if you did not explore the magnificent 15th century 'wool' church and walk around this picturesque and fascinating town, this is your opportunity to do so.

# TOUR 10 – COLOURFUL CHARACTERS

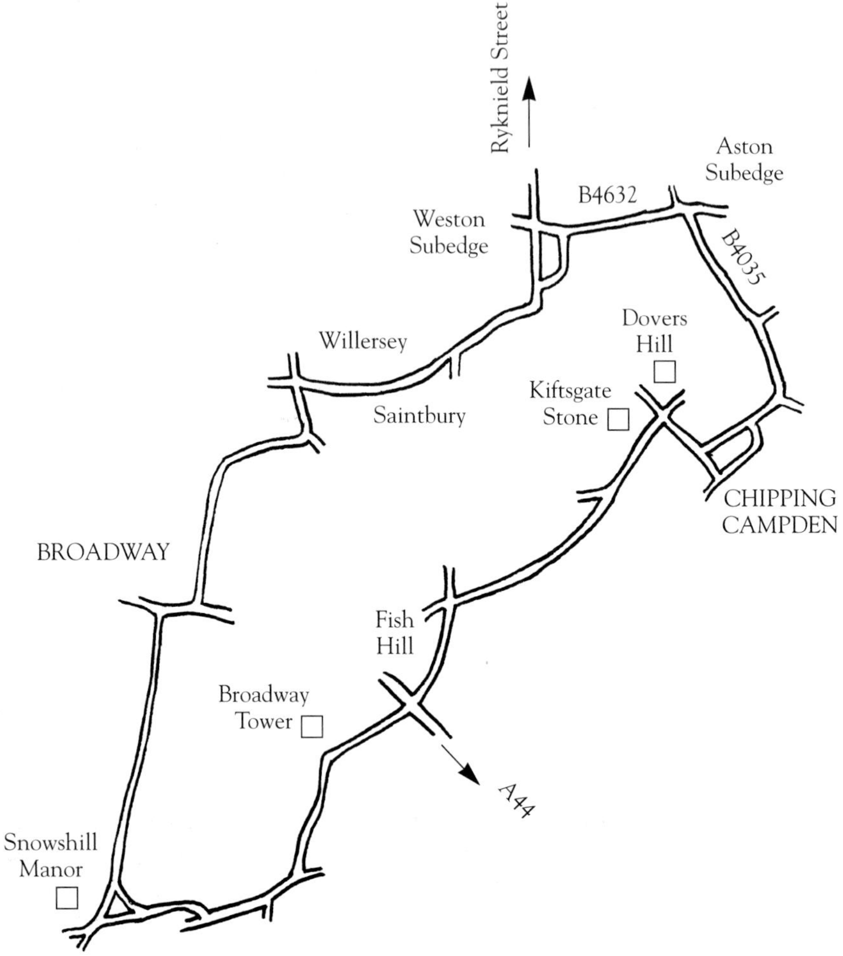

Rykneild Street

Aston
Subedge

B4632

Weston
Subedge

B4035

Willersey

Dovers
Hill

Kiftsgate
Stone

Saintbury

CHIPPING
CAMPDEN

BROADWAY

Fish
Hill

Broadway
Tower

A44

Snowshill
Manor

# DIRECTIONS:

*After visiting the town, leave Chipping Campden on the B4035 which takes you down the steep escarpment to Aston Subedge. Turn left here onto the busier B4632 through Weston Subedge, Willersey and Broadway. At Broadway turn right into the main street (direction Cheltenham). Leave the village following National Trust signs to Snowshill Manor on the village green – it is 2¹/₂mls up the steep, narrow hill to the manor house but parking is well organised. After your visit continue up hill, and bear left following signs for Chipping Campden (5¹/₂mls). This straight open road brings you to the approach road to Broadway Tower (on the left). Follow this down to the tower and it will bring you round in a loop back just before the busy A44. Cross straight over the main road following signs for Saintbury picnic area at Fish Hill (ignore the sign right to Chipping Campden) and continue, past the Kiftsgate Stone in the woods to the left, to a minor cross roads. The National Trust observation point at Dover Hill is signposted to the left here. Returning to this crossroads, Chipping Campden is straight across and down the hill.*

# APPROX. DISTANCE: 18 miles

# RECOMMENDED:

*The Noel Arms Hotel, Volunteer Inn, Kings Arms Hotel, Chipping Campden; Seagrave Arms, Weston Subedge; Bell Inn, Willersey; Lygon Arms Hotel, Swan Inn, Broadway Hotel, Crown & Trumpet Inn, Hunters Lodge, Broadway; Snowshill Arms, Snowshill.*

*Market Hall (1627), Chipping Campden.*

CHIPPING CAMPDEN is steeped in history. It is picturesque-enough to be a film set. Stand under the dusty timbers of the Market Hall and gaze out at the quaint town houses, the old coaching inns and the sun dials – there seems to be one on every house. Sir Baptist Hicks, who built the Market Hall, and the row of Almshouses, also built the great house which stood beside the church. It was destroyed in the Civil War and only its exotic-looking gatehouses and lodges remain. You can see his magnificent tomb in the great 'wool' church, where he and his wife Elizabeth are splendidly depicted in alabaster ruffs and silks. Sir Baptist Hicks became so rich that he was able to lend the king huge sums of money and was rewarded with the title Viscount Campden the year before his death in 1629.

The town's first great benefactor was William Grevel, said to be one of the richest wool merchants in England, who died in 1401. His house with its distinctive two-storey bay window stands in the main street and his memorial brass can be seen in the chancel of the church which he helped build. You can visit the WOOLSTAPLERS HALL MUSEUM in the High Street (Open daily Apr-Oct, 10.00-5.00. Admission Charge. Tel: 01386-840289) and see the interior of medieval wool merchant, Robert Calf's house which dates from about 1340. C. R. Ashbee who brought the Guild of Handicrafts from London's East End lived here from 1902-1911 and was

*William Grevel's house (late 14th century), Chipping Campden.*

*Gateway to Campden Manor (c. 1613), Chipping Campden.*

85

responsible for the restoration of the house. The museum contains a weird and wonderful collection of memorabilia and bric-a-brac, much of it local. The tourist office has its premises on the ground floor of the building.

Leaving Chipping Campden we descend the sharp hill of the limestone escarpment: pretty ASTON SUBEDGE lies at the bottom, 'under the edge'. A fine half timbered farmhouse by the road and the abundant orchards of the area make us realise that we are in the Vale of Evesham. To the right of the road is the manor house where Endymion Porter lived. Porter, born in 1587, was an ambassador at the time of Charles I and bought pictures for the king on the continent. He was a generous patron of the arts and lifelong friend of the poet Robert Herrick.

WESTON SUBEDGE is equally charming. Roman Ryknield Street – from Stow to Alcester – runs beside the village. Turn off the main road by the Seagrave Arms pub to discover the heart of the village and the church. William Latimer was the scholar who translated Aristotle from the Latin and inaugurated the teaching of Greek at Oxford. He was also a great friend of William Tyndale (SEE TOUR 9), Linacre and Erasmus, and 'Latimers' in the village was his home. He was buried in 1545 in neighbouring SAINTBURY where he was also vicar. If you only have time for one church, Saintbury is probably the most interesting in this particular group.

WILLERSEY comes next in the line of villages which were founded at the foot of the ridge because of the abundant springs gushing out at the base of the inferior oolite rock. In spring the woods around Willersey are carpeted with wild daffodils. William Roper, who lived in the manor here, became Sir Thomas More's son-in-law when he married his daughter Margaret.

BROADWAY has altogether more substance than the previous villages and is very much on the tourist trail. The Cotswold stone here has a mellow, almost orange tone, and the village houses group elegantly around the green. William Morris was entranced with Broadway and encouraged a steady stream of literary and artistic visitors to the village. John Singer Sargent spent several blissful summers painting scenes in the garden of Russell House which he and some artistic friends leased in 1885. Even Henry James approved of Broadway enthusing that 'everything is stone except the greenness'. Today Broadway is still a place of pilgrimage for American tourists who adore the rather expensive antique shops and rightly rave about the picturesque and luxurious Lygon Arms Hotel. Don't miss Gordon Russell's showroom for his highly collectable handmade furniture in the Arts & Craft tradition of the Cotswolds.

From Broadway we climb up to SNOWSHILL on a narrow, steep road

out of the village. Although the manor itself is small and idyllically situated nestling into the side of the hill, parking and facilities associated with large numbers of visitors are well organised. SNOWSHILL MANOR (Open May-Sept daily except Tues 1.00-6.00; Apr & Oct, Sat & Sun only 1.00-5.00. Admission Charge. Tel: 01386-852410) houses the bizarre and fascinating collection of a very wealthy eccentric, Charles Paget Wade.

Inheriting the family fortune from sugar plantations in St. Kitts, Wade bought Snowshill Manor in 1919 on impulse, having seen its photograph in an old Country Life magazine while serving in France in the First World War. He lived without electric light, or any of the usual modern conveniences, in the adjoining Priests' House as his collection grew and grew. He filled the rooms of his manor house, each of which bears a name – Admiral, Zenith, Hundred Wheels, etc., with such an amazing variety of objects, many of which he repaired himself (his coat of arms proclaims 'Let Nothing Perish'), that it is hard to say what his true passions were. Suffice it to say that Snowshill has collections of bicycles, Samurai armour, model ships, beetles, musical instruments and oriental furniture. It also has peaceful gardens, inspiring views and a welcoming pub next door to the manor house.

*Broadway Tower.*

On the top of the hill above Broadway, and visible for miles around, stands a very grand tower built in 1800 for the Earl of Coventry's second wife. After lighting experimental beacons to ascertain the feasibility of the enterprise, the earl went ahead with a more permanent structure – 1000 feet above sea level, one room on each floor, and 74 steps up the tower – which could be seen miles away at his wife's family home, Croome Court in Worcestershire.

BROADWAY TOWER (Open daily Apr-Oct 10.00-6.00. Admission Charge. Tel: 01386-852390) has spectacular views over a great many counties, 12 at the moment although it has been 14. A small collection of memorabilia recalls the summer holiday William Morris and his pre-Raphaelite friends spent at the tower. There are also exhibits relating to the local wool industry and the history of the tower. The tower now stands in its own COUNTRY PARK with an adventure playground as well as a colourful selection of animals including Red Deer and blue pygmy goats.

Our final stop is at Dovers Hill just above Chipping Campden. But about 300 yards or so before the cross roads and its sign to Dovers Hill, you may care to search for the famous KIFTSGATE STONE in the woods beside the road. The massive standing stone was used as a rallying point for the men of the Kiftsgate "Hundred' in Saxon times, but it had probably been standing by track along the ridge for quite a while before that.

The dramatic viewpoint at DOVERS HILL was bought by the National Trust in 1928. An engraved brass dial points out the landmarks of the panorama while information boards recount the history of the Cotswold Olympic Games. Amazingly the games are still held, in June each year, but they are a pale shadow of the boistrous, uproarious, often violent revelry of the original competitions. Shin-kicking was particularly popular, with contestants preparing their ankles by battering them with planks and other hard objects for weeks before the event. There was also fierce competition in 'Jumping in Bags', cudgel-beating, and leaping, as well as a 'Jingling Match' – whatever that was. Inevitably there were horseraces, and gambling, and before long the games were so popular that 30,000 people were attending.

The man behind the Cotswold Olympic Games was one Robert Dover, who through the offices of his courtier acquaintance Endymion Porter (see page 89), managed to obtain James I's permission to hold the annual event. The first games was held in 1604, and for the next 40 years Robert Dover opened the games on a splendid white horse wearing a magnificent yellow silk suit and feathered hat belonging to the King. The Civil War which saw the destruction of Campden House and much else in the Cotswolds caused the games to cease for a while, but they revived with the Restoration and continued until they finally became so roudy and violent that they were stopped by the local vicar in 1851.

We return to Chipping Campden following the path of the Scuttlebrook Wake when the weary contestants and villagers process back down in costume to the square for the fair, the dancing and the ox-roast. Should you be in the Cotswolds in June, Chipping Campden, watched over by the shades of Robert Dover and Endymion Porter, is the place to be.

# TOURIST INFORMATION CENTRES IN THE COTSWOLDS:

CHELTENHAM SPA
Municipal Offices, 77 Promenade
Tel: 01242-522878

STOW-ON-THE-WOLD
Hollis House, The Square
Tel: 01451-831082

CHIPPING CAMPDEN*
Woolstaplers' Hall Museum,
High Street
Tel: 01386-840289

STROUD
Subscription rooms,
Kendrick Street
Tel: 01453-765768

CIRENCESTER
Corn Hall, Market Place
Tel: 01285-654180

TETBURY*
Old Court House, 63 Long Street
Tel: 01666-503552

NORTHLEACH*
Cotswolds Countryside Collection
Tel: 01451-860715

WINCHCOMBE*
The Town Hall, High Street
Tel: 01242-602925

*Seasonal opening only.

# ACKNOWLEDGEMENTS

Tizzie Knowles and Geoffrey Lintott for their delightful pen and ink drawings.

Angela Mason whose sheep figure so prominently in the Cotswolds and in this book.

The Corinium Museum, Cirencester, for the loan of their photograph by Tim Bryce on page 13.

All other photographs by the author.

**S.B. Publications** publish a wide range of local interest books.
For a list of titles in print write (enclosing S.A.E.) to:-
S.B. Publications, c/o 19 Grove Road, Seaford, East Sussex BN25 1TP.